THE ADOPTION LIFE CYCLE

THE
ADOPTION
LIFE CYCLE

The Children and Their Families Through the Years

ELINOR B. ROSENBERG

THE FREE PRESS

A Division of Macmillan, Inc.
New York

Maxwell Macmillan Canada
Toronto

Maxwell Macmillan International
New York   Oxford   Singapore   Sydney

The Free Press
A Division of Macmillan, Inc.
866 Third Avenue, New York, N.Y. 10022

Maxwell Macmillan Canada, Inc.
1200 Eglinton Avenue East
Suite 200
Don Mills, Ontario M3C 3N1

Macmillan, Inc. is part of the Maxwell Communication Group of Companies.

Printed in the United States of America

printing number

2   3   4   5   6   7   8   9   10

Library of Congress Cataloging-in-Publication Data

Rosenberg, Elinor B.
    The adoption life cycle: the children and their families through
the years/Elinor B. Rosenberg.
        p. cm.
    ISBN 0-02-927055-3
    1. Adoption—United States—Psychological aspects.
    2. Developmental psychology—United States.   3. Life cycle, Human.
I. Title.
HV875.55.R66   1992
362.7′34′019—dc20   92-9031
                                                                          CIP

To my children

PETER MORRIS ROSENBERG

and

SARAH LYNN ROSENBERG

CONTENTS

PREFACE

MY INTRODUCTION TO THE WORLD OF ADOPTION occurred in 1962 when I was assigned to work at the Booth Memorial Hospital's Home for Unwed Mothers in Boston, my first fieldwork placement in the master's program at Simmons College School of Social Work. There I worked with women and their families from early pregnancy through delivery and relinquishment. I heard from some of these women for years afterward—usually on their baby's birthday. The birth mothers I had contact with represented a full range of socioeconomic backgrounds, personalities, and family dynamics. There were some women who I thought were healthy, well-functioning people and others who appeared to be significantly disturbed; the majority were somewhere in between. The event of the unplanned pregnancy and relinquishment seemed to have a different meaning in each case.

My first professional positions were in residential treatment centers for children. There I came into contact with a disproportionate number of adopted children and their families. In those days (1964–1966) there was little literature on adoption, and the prevailing spirit was that adoption posed no special problems. As I worked with these families, however, many questions came to mind about the special issues adoptees and their families faced. These questions were still unanswered when my husband and I adopted our son and then our daughter as infants in 1966 and 1968.

To explore these questions further, in the early 1970s I consulted with Humberto Nagera, a child analyst in the Child Psychiatry Department at the University of Michigan, where I also worked. Dr. Nagera introduced me to the idea that there is an alternative developmental course for adoptees. "Adoptive parents will sweat more with their children," he said. I later recognized this as a generous piece of wisdom.

For the next 20 years I watched our family grow and observed other adoptive families in the community and in clinical settings. At the same time, a significant literature on adoption began to appear. Through my own professional and personal experience and through reports of others, it became clear that being involved in an adoption posed significant challenges to birth parents, adoptive parents, and adoptees—that is, to all members of the adoption circle. For some, these challenges are highly charged and are a driving force in their lives. For others, they remain background sounds. There is also a natural ebb and flow as issues related to adoption emerge at significant times and recede at others. I began to see how these challenges are posed in the context of human development and that adoption circle members adapt and cope with the challenges throughout the entire life cycle.

As part of the preparation for writing this book, I became more acquainted with adoption activist groups and with current adoption-related legal and social systems, of which I had some awareness but little personal experience. I enthusiastically signed up for a local conference on adoption and took my place with a group of 200 participants. I liked the idea that all members of the adoption circle were sitting together to discuss mutual concerns. At one point the moderator called for a show of hands of birth parents, adoptive parents, and adoptees. There was a quiet noting of the numbers of birth parents and adoptees and then an awkward smattering of applause for the adoptive parents. This puzzled me. There was a similar occurrence when we divided into workshops: the woman behind me whispered ''Bless your heart'' when I raised my hand to be counted with the other adoptive parents. Throughout the presentation and, later, the discussion period, I became aware of a phenomenon of which I had been totally ignorant; it was apparent that the struggles of adoptive parents were seen as qualitatively different from those of birth parents and adoptees. The awkward applause and blessings were expressions of an ambivalent appreciation that those who were most advantaged would show enough concern about the others to attend such a meeting. There were some who saw adoptive parents as the exploiters of birth parents and adoptees. There are clearly powerful political crosscurrents swirling in the adoption circle. Observing this phenomenon further inspired me to write about how I see the adoption circle as an interrelated system, with birth parents, adoptive parents, and adoptees being a significant presence in each other's lives throughout all their years.

Following a presentation of life cycle issues in adoption at the University of Michigan, my colleague Morton Chethik breezed by and commented to me, "You have a book there, you know." I have since both credited and blamed him for the idea of writing this book. Many friends, colleagues, and family members have helped me in the process of writing it, and I want to thank them all.

Fady Hajal and his research group at the Cornell Medical Center contributed to the original conceptualization of life cycle issues in adoption. The staff of the University Center for the Child and the Family at the University of Michigan participated in further discussions of these conceptual issues. Members of the 1991 Family Therapy Seminar in Child Psychiatry at the University of Michigan indulged me by devoting an entire semester of meetings to my material. The members of the seminar were Bob Cohen, Susan Darrow, Joshua Ehrlich, Brenda Holt, Kathy MacDonald, Frances Shakleford, and Bennett Wolper. They all actively affected the shape of this work. Barbara Cain, Marilyn Young, Sharon Wittenberg, Joshua Ehrlich, Thomas Horner, Margaret Buttenheim, Neil Kalter, Joan Hollinger, and Peter Rosenberg all read parts of the book and provided helpful comments, for which I am very grateful. Suzanne Mosher Ferguson has offered warm support and helpful pieces of advice at crucial moments. Susan Arellano of The Free Press was a keen critic and was enormously helpful in keeping the book grounded and geared to the reader. I am grateful to Paulette Lockwood and to Carol Rolph for their expert typing and for their patience with my archaic snip-and-paste method of revision.

Andrea Adler has offered the best of professional help and friendship from the moment I first toyed with the idea of writing this book, through its frustrating times, and up to its completion, patiently reading draft after draft. She had the uncanny ability to phone me on the very days I had decided to give up book writing and urge me on, although I still doubt it is true that she has a number of friends who are postponing decisions about adoption until they read this book. Her insights and support were major contributants to this work for which I will always be grateful.

My husband, Bill Rosenberg, took my work seriously long before I did. His faith in my endeavors has taken many forms. As

a companion in this adventure he has advised, coached, pro-
voked, and cajoled me. We have been partners in learning to be
adoptive parents. In all of this, he has been my dearest friend.

My children, Peter and Sarah, began contributing to this book
the day we brought each of them home. They have taught me
about their experiences and have helped me better understand
my own. Each has helped me learn the rewards of mastering necessary tasks and has enriched my life in ways they may never
fully understand.

I set out to write the book I wish had been available to Bill
and me, to our children, to their birth parents, to therapists, and
others involved in the world of adoption. It does not address all
circumstances, nor does it provide specific answers. I hope its
principles are applicable and useful to the many individuals and
families who live in and around the adoption circle.

I have organized this book to best meet the needs of a range of
readers. Each chapter is designed to be free standing. The developmental tasks of birth parents, adoptive parents, and adoptees
are presented separately with some commentary on their overlap-
ping issues. Their interrelationships are focused upon in chapter
5. The chapter in clinical interventions is technical in approach
and incorporates the developmental material. The final discussion of legal and social implications is based on the developmental and interactional conceptualization throughout the book.
I hope this organization enables readers to use this as a resource
book as well as an integrated presentation of significant issues of
adoption.

CHAPTER 1

THE MYTH OF THE PERFECT SOLUTION

IN 1971 LISA AND JONATHAN W. APPLIED to adopt a child from a highly respected agency in New York City. A year later they brought home a beautiful baby girl they named Jennifer Louise. They were overjoyed to have this child and were also pleased to hear that the child's birth mother was delighted with the placement. The agency offered the adoptive and birth parents little information about each other. The name on the birth certificate was rewritten as Jennifer W., and the original was placed under court seal. The agency social worker assured Lisa and Jonathan that this child, like all others, simply needed a secure home with loving parents. No problems were anticipated.

At that time, adoption of children was commonly thought to be the perfect solution to a myriad of problems: birth parents who chose to continue a pregnancy but could not raise their child could expect the child to be well cared for and supported; infertile couples who longed for a child were able to fulfill their wishes for a family; fertile couples who chose to enlarge their families while meeting a social need could do so; children who needed parents were provided with a welcoming home; and child welfare agents in the legal, social, and medical systems were able to offer a solution that, for once, was opposed by no one. The social institution of adoption seemed to meet the needs of all members of what we now call the adoption circle—birth parents, adoptive parents, and adoptees—and the social and legal systems that surround them.

But did it? At the annual meeting of the American Adoption Congress in 1991 two well-known spokespersons in the field argued emphatically that it did not.[1] They called, instead, for an end to the practice of adoption entirely, declaring that adoption by nonrelatives simply does not work and that completely new arrangements should be made for the care of children in need.

It has become apparent over the years that what was once thought to be a problem with an obvious and simple solution in fact involves a very complicated process. The needs of birth parents, adoptive parents, and adoptees are not completely met with the mutual signing of an adoption agreement. Rather, all members of the adoption circle deal with important issues related to this agreement over the course of their entire lifetimes.

In order to even begin to form an opinion regarding the viability of different kinds of adoption contracts, we need to understand the lifelong experiences of all members of the adoption circle, with all their pleasures, pain, hopes, wishes, and conflicts. We need to see the ways in which their existences interact and impact upon each other in the course of their lifetimes. Only with this understanding can we assess the success of adoption as a social institution in comparison with its real alternatives: birthparents raising a child they feel ill-prepared to parent, children being raised by parents in such circumstances, and potential adoptive parents remaining childless.

We get glimpses of the lives of members of the adoption circle through public media and our own personal experiences. The issues they face present themselves as brief moments in time, snapshots whose meaning often has many levels, some of which may elude us. For example, we turn on the five o'clock news and witness the reunion of a birth mother with the 28-year-old son she placed for adoption in infancy. While friends and family observe them through tearful eyes, mother and child embrace and whisper, "I've always loved you." The reporter describes the long, hard search of the adoptee, his almost lifelong feeling of incompleteness and desire to know his roots. The birth mother is interviewed. She tells of her 28-year grief as she thought of her son each day and lit candles on each of his birthdays, wishing he would come home to her. Birth mother and son are ecstatic at the reunion and make plans to continue seeing each other. The report does not mention the adoptive parents, what part they played in the search, and what feelings they have had about it. In this scene they are as ghostlike as the birth mother was for the first 28 years of the son's life. What does this mean? Does it mean that the birth mother is the "real" mother after all? Has the young man been unhappy all his 28 years? Does it mean that the adoptive parents did not provide a good enough home? Does it mean there can be "time sharing" in an adoptive family?

What is graphically clear from this reunion scene is that the birth mother and the adoptee have experienced significant grief over the loss of each other. What is not clear is whether this was a necessary loss, how such a loss can be coped with, and what the quality of their respective lives would have been had the birth mother kept and raised her son.

But descriptions of the grieved, searching birth mother are not the only ones we hear. As we open the morning paper and scan "Dear Abby," we see a letter that reads:

Dear Abby: When I was 16, I became pregnant out of wedlock. I was so ashamed that I told no one. When I was four months along, I told my parents, who were very loving and understanding. I was sent to live with my grandmother in another state and stayed with her until I graduated from high school. No one in the family knew about this pregnancy except for my grandmother and my parents—not even my siblings were told. In those days, a pregnancy out of wedlock was a terrible disgrace so I gave my baby up for adoption.

Over 20 years have passed and now my most horrible nightmare has come true. I received a letter from the adoption agency wanting to know of my whereabouts. The letter was sent to my parents' home in a state where I no longer reside. They are as devastated by this invasion of privacy as I.

Abby, I gave the child up for adoption in order to close that chapter in my life and I do not want to be located. So far, I have done nothing about answering the letter from the agency because I don't know where to turn. Fear is consuming me and it's making me sick. Had I known this could happen, I may have chosen another option. Please tell me what course of action to take. (signed) "Closed Chapter."

Abby at first replies: "Have a lawyer write to the adoption agency and advise it that you gave up the child for adoption with the understanding that your identity and whereabouts were not to be disclosed. And that's the way you want it." Later, in response to readers' objections, she revises her advice and writes:

> The overwhelming number of letters I received from my readers caused me to make a partial turnaround on this one. I now realize that the adoptee has a right to know all the facts concerning his or her birth family, and the opportunity to meet them should be made available if all parties are willing. The secrecy that shrouded adoption is no longer necessary now that society has come to understand that "illegitimate pregnancy" is not an unforgivable crime.*

What is being implied about the birth mother who signs herself "Closed Chapter"? How is she different from the one we saw on the five o'clock news? Does she not have normal maternal instincts? Is she too self-protective? What effect will her refusal have on her searching child? Should "Closed Chapter" forfeit her privacy and expose herself to pain for the sake of her child's interests? Are Abby's readers correct that the adoptee has a right to know the facts of the birth family? Does the child's right to information supersede the birth mother's right to privacy?

In her own news column, Ann Landers responded differently to a letter raising similar questions. She held the position that adoptees have the right to know about their *health history only* and insists that they do not have the right "to intrude into the lives of people who do not want the past raked up and wish to be left alone." Additionally, she believes that women who placed their children for adoption have no right to look for those children later and "demand a relationship."[2]

These letters clearly illustrate marked differences among the experiences of birth mothers: some women are eager for information about or actual contact with their children while others wish for continued confidentiality. These letters also illustrate divergence in public opinion regarding who has what rights. Some

---

*Taken from the *Dear Abby* column by Abigail Van Buren. Copyright 1990 Universal Press Syndicate. Reprinted with permission. All rights reserved. The articles appeared on October 23 and November 27, 1990.

maintain that the original contract of confidentiality is sacrosanct and no one has a right to open any sealed record. Others approve of variations of rights to identifying or nonidentifying information, sometimes where there is mutual agreement and sometimes where there is not. The question of rights has important social and legal implications.

Adoptive parents also have their own issues to face. We talk to a 50-year-old friend who has three adopted children, all of whom have developed well and with whom she enjoys good relationships. She has just been to a baby shower for a friend and finds herself feeling both sad and envious. "I don't understand this," she says, weeping. "I am genuinely happy for Karen, and I feel very fully gratified by my own children. I love them, I enjoy them, I feel very lucky to have them. I don't even want to have any more. So why do I feel so envious of Karen's pregnancy, and why do I feel so sad that I've never been pregnant? It doesn't make any sense. I must be crazy."

Is she crazy? Is it crazy to wish for a pregnancy when you don't even want another baby? Does this mean that adopting children doesn't really "work" for parents, that they never really get what they most want? Again, these questions can only be answered in a lifetime developmental context. Fifty-year-old women face menopause and the clear ending of their childbearing years. Each woman says good-bye to that phase of life in her own way. A woman who has not actually borne children says good-bye to the fantasy that it could still happen and grieves the loss of that fantasy, yet her pleasure in parenting is still real and rich.

Like all parents, adoptive parents have to cope with their children's difficulties in growing up. We hear of one set of adoptive parents who refer their 13-year-old son for psychotherapy after he is apprehended by the police for shoplifting a pencil from the local mall. The parents had begun to notice a pattern in which their son would get into trouble each year around his birthday. They had previously attributed this behavior to excitement about the birthday, but now wonder if this "excitement" is actually anxiety. As the boy works with his therapist, it becomes clear that birthdays are highly charged times in which he thinks about his birth mother and wonders if she is thinking of him, too. He hopes she is and also hopes that she wants to come and take him back to her. At the same time, he loves his adoptive parents and would never want to leave them, so it makes him scared to think that the birth mother might actually come to get him. Afraid of hurting his parents' feelings by sharing his own, he keeps them to himself. He thinks of himself as a bad "throwaway" baby and as a disloyal adoptive son. These feelings of "badness" become expressed symbolically in the "bad" shoplifting behavior. The trouble he feels within himself is translated into trouble in the community.

What are we to think about this boy and his family? Would he not be thinking about his birth mother if he "really" loved his adoptive parents? Does it speak poorly of them that he didn't want to tell them about his feelings? Do adopted children get into more trouble than their nonadopted counterparts? It is apparent that this youngster is having to confront issues that are directly related to his being adopted, issues that are particularly salient as he reaches puberty and questions his identity. While his struggle presents problems to himself and those around him, it can also be seen as part of a natural and expectable process as he attempts to master these emotional tasks that are specific to adopted people.

In recent years, children with special needs have increasingly become candidates for adoption rather than remaining in foster care or in institutions. For example, Suzy, a plucky 11-year-old was returned to the court by her adoptive parents. This young girl had survived a violent family background: at three years of age she witnessed her father kill her mother. After her mother's death she was placed in a foster home along with her siblings. There, for two years, she seemed anxious and behaved in an irritable and provocative manner. She was then placed with an adoptive family who had already adopted a child who was adjusting well. The adoptive parents had been assured by the child placement agency that Suzy would settle down from her anxiety once she was in a permanent, loving home. But Suzy never became calm and never became attached to the family, even though they attached to her. In fact, as time went on, she became increasingly agitated and presented behavior problems of escalating seriousness. She lied, stole, destroyed family treasures, and set fires. The adoptive family took her to behavior specialists and twice had to hospitalize her. Therapists who worked with her and with her family came to understand that Suzy tenaciously maintained the belief that she was responsible for her mother's death. She was terrified of becoming close to anyone for fear of also causing them harm. The adoptive family's efforts to be warm and close to her only made her want to distance herself from them with bad behavior. Despite intensive therapeutic intervention, she seemed unable to live in an emotionally close family.

Feeling exhausted and depleted of resources, Suzy's parents went to court for a release from the adoption. Although they could no longer parent Suzy, they hoped to keep in touch with her in subsequent years in order to offer continued emotional and financial support. The presiding judge approved the release but berated the couple for reneging on their commitment to the child. He cited them as failures at making up for Suzy's early life experiences. Was it their fault that the adoption failed? If they had been different people, could Suzy have adjusted?

Currently, a growing number of "special needs" children are available for adoption; the national number doubled from 1984 to 1987. Studies show that 10%–15% of these adoptions fall apart even before they are finalized.[3] It has become apparent that these children need far more than a loving, stable home. There is often a need for extensive services, including support and counseling for the adoptive parents, who are required to develop special skills in raising children with special needs.

Prospective parents seeking healthy infants or other children often explore all available options. Magazine and newspaper articles that discuss the "baby business" describe prospective adoptive parents' struggles to find available children through licensed agencies and through individual facilitators on both a national and international basis. We hear of experiences that are wonderful success stories and others that are heartbreaking nightmares. Fees for services range from subsidies for "hard to place" children to a cost to the adoptive parents of 20 or 30 thousand dollars for healthy white infants. Should a child be removed from his national origins? What is a reasonable fee for placement of a child? Does the exchange of money really reflect the buying and selling of children?

The timing and content of the disclosure of adoptive status to children has also been the subject of much controversy. In her autobiography Kitty Dukakis, wife of 1988 presidential candidate Michael Dukakis, blames her family's secrecy concerning her mother's adoption for her long history of low self-esteem and for much of her own alcohol and drug addiction.[4] When she was 18, Mrs. Dukakis learned from a cousin that her mother had been adopted, and she later learned that her mother was illegitimate. Mrs. Dukakis reports feeling "thunderstruck" on learning that her grandparents were, in fact, her mother's adoptive parents and that a condition of the adoption had been that the birth mother be allowed to live in the household as a nanny to her child. Mrs. Dukakis tells of experiencing the revelation as an enormous breach of trust and indicates that this traumatic moment, which has haunted her for years, marked the beginning of a 26-year addiction to alcohol and amphetamines.

What does this story tell us? Would a breach of trust in any form have produced this degree of trauma, or is it specific to the adoption issue? Was Mrs. Dukakis's distress due to the misrepresentation of actual kinship status? The broken genealogical link might have been manageable had she been told at an age when she could understand the difference between the biological and adoptive relationships and could begin to consider the arrangement as an effort to most adequately provide for her mother's well-being.

We see pictures in the media of demonstrations in which participants are demanding that adoption records be opened. Demonstrators in the annual march on Washington, begun in 1989, have stated that "determined people are marching for adoptees' rights to know who they are and for birth parents' rights to know where their sons and daughters are." Other groups maintain a belief in the need for and right to confidentiality for all members of the adoption circle. They want adoption practices to remain as they were originally established and strongly support adoption over abortion.

In 1990 Lincoln Caplan published a book entitled *An Open Adoption* in which he describes the experiences of a birth mother and adoptive parents who meet, choose each other, and plan to have open contact and communication throughout the child's lifetime.[5] Is this a solution to the social, emotional, and legal problems related to confidentiality? Answers vary widely.

These snapshots of the adoption circle offer us some glimpses of the kinds of issues birth parents, adoptive parents, and adoptees confront as they navigate their course through life. We are now so mired in confusion and controversy, it is hard to remember that adoption is as old as family life itself and, with the story of Moses in the bulrushes, even recorded in the Bible. Was it always so complicated, confusing, and conflictual? By looking briefly at the history of adoption as a social institution, we can see more clearly how we reached the state we are in and perhaps begin to see our way toward more effective practices.

THE HISTORY OF ADOPTION

All societies in all times have had to find ways of dealing with children whose biological parents are unable to provide for them. Before the 19th century care for such children was most commonly arranged on an informal basis. Families absorbed needful children without legal or social interventions. However, families tended not to welcome children born of unwed mothers: their births were so shrouded with shame that efforts were made to dispense with them in order to protect the mother's reputation. In the 17th and 18th centuries such children were placed in foundling homes provided by the state. Those who survived infancy were exploited in the labor force; some were placed on "orphan trains" and transported to the countryside where farmers and their wives would choose healthy-looking children and adopt them to use as field hands.

The industrial revolution interrupted the indenturing of children, which had been the basis of informal adoption, and adoption laws were developed. These laws reflected a new value on protecting the welfare of children. In 1851 Massachusetts established the first adoption statute designed to safeguard the rights of children, a statute that included control of adoption. Charitable organizations continued to arrange for children's care and reflected the religious or moral beliefs of the group. In 1912 the United States Children's Bureau was established as the first public child welfare agency. Both private adoptions (which are arranged by a facilitator, often a physician or lawyer, who matches birth parents with adopting couples) and agency adoptions have continued from that time to the present.

From the 1940s until the mid-1980s, agency adoptions were practiced in a confidential (usually termed "closed" or "traditional") manner in the United States. Adoptive parents and birth parents had no contact; they were given minimal information about each other. The birth records were rewritten as if the child had been born to the adoptive parents. The authentic records were placed under court seal; they were to be opened only in a life-or-death situation, such as a medical intervention requiring a blood relative. The original reasoning behind this policy was to protect adopted children from knowledge of their immoral conception and reflected a shift from viewing illegitimate children as being tainted by "bad blood" to conceptualizing them as tabulae rasae who should be protected from untoward experiences. The principle of protecting the unwed mother's secret so that she could go on to live an upstanding life continued. In 1955 a national conference on adoption sponsored by the Child Welfare League of America set the stage for reforms in practice that reflected an orientation toward the "best interests of the child." It was believed that confidentiality in adoption served these interests by providing an atmosphere in which adopted children were treated as if they had been born into the adoptive family. This was the era in which adoption was viewed as the perfect solution.

What seemed perfect about this solution then was that it appeared to meet the needs of all participants equally well. Birth parents were relieved of their burden, adoptive parents were provided with the child they longed for, and children got the welcoming homes they needed. Adoption practices supported the "as if" quality of this alternative family structure: it was as if the birth mother had never borne this child, as if the adoptive mother herself had. Members of the social service and legal agencies surrounding the families enjoyed their matchmaking function and the relief and pleasure their services provided. In finalizing an adoption of an infant in the late 1960s, one juvenile court judge commented that this was the only part of his job that brought him real pleasure. What happened that made people question whether these practices really met everyone's needs, as had been believed?

The social and sexual revolution of the 1960s, the development of more effective birth control measures, and the legitimization of abortion in the 1970s all had a profound effect on adoption practices. Pregnancies were more frequently prevented or aborted; women felt less social stigma about sexuality outside of marriage and more frequently kept their unplanned babies. With a diminished supply of relinquished babies, private adoption practices soared. At the same time, some of the basic social and psychosocial beliefs that supported the "as if" quality of the adoptive family system began to change. One important shift was away from the belief in the predominance of nurture over nature as an influence on individual development. During the era of adoption as a perfect solution, there was a conceptualization of a newborn baby as a blank slate whose impressions would come primarily from the environment. New information about genetic structure and heredity shifted this view so that both nature and nurture were seen as influential, the balance different for each individual.

This new knowledge required everyone to consider more seriously the issues of biology.

Another important psychosocial shift was from the valuing of the homogeneity deriving from the melting pot ideal to a valuing of individual and ethnic differences. Alex Haley's presentation of the importance of roots and identity in 1976 captured and crystallized this phenomenon.[6] The Black Pride Movement gave other ethnic groups permission to acknowledge and take pleasure in their ethnicity and to explore their roots.

A third shift occurred as a result of the popularization of psychological literature. Loss and grieving became popular topics, and support for the lifting of repressed thoughts and feelings grew dramatically. There was strong encouragement for saying what one really thought and for expressing innermost thoughts openly and finding one's true identity.

All these shifts challenged the concept of adoption as a perfect solution and raised questions about existing adoption practices. There was a movement toward transracial and transcultural adoption as well as toward adoption of children previously labeled unadoptable. The range of adoptive parents expanded to include unmarried and gay people. All members of the adoption circle began to question the value of confidentiality, with many birth parents and adoptees seeing it as an infringement of their civil rights.

There are now large advocacy organizations and support groups formed by adoptees, adoptive parents, and birth parents. Most groups seek some reform of adoption laws and practice. For example, Concerned United Birth Parents (CUB) is a nonprofit organization based in Des Moines that advocates the opening of adoption records to adoptees and recommends an acceptance of two sets of parents, similar to stepparent and foster home arrangements. CUB espouses a primary goal of avoiding unnecessary adoptions and keeping biological families together. The American Adoption Congress, a national organization of adoptee support groups, also advocates opening adoption records to adoptees. On the other hand, the National Committee for Adoption, a nonprofit organization based in Washington, D.C., takes a different position and advocates the maintenance of confidentiality for birth parents and for adoptive parents. Thirty-five states have set up a joint registry system enabling birth parents and adult adoptees to meet if both consent. While state legislators consider the creation of registries a significant reform in adoption law, many adoptee activists believe this is a violation of their civil rights and oppose it because it allows the control of adoptee–birth parent contacts to remain in the hands of the state rather than in the hands of the individual who feels entitled to this information. They object to a system where birth parents can say no to their child's request for contact. The rights of adoptees and birth parents thus remain a contested issue.

Recent reforms in the adoption movement aim to modify or replace policies of confidentiality with more openness or cooperation between adoptive parents and birth parents. Since the mid-1980s agencies in some states (for example, Texas, California, and Michigan) have practiced more openness in adoption. Birth parents and adoptive parents can be given extensive information about each other, and birth parents can take an active role in the selection of their child's adoptive parents. In such cases the birth parents and prospective adoptive parents may meet each other and determine how much and what kind of contact the birth parents will have over the course of the child's life. Some agree to written communications only, some to periodic visits, and some to regular ongoing contacts.

Objections to open or cooperative adoptions are raised on several grounds. Some critics express concern about a child's ability to manage relationships with two sets of parents, fearing the ability to bond and feel grounded in a family is compromised by this arrangement.[7] They also question whether adoptive parents can sufficiently bond to the child[8] and whether birth parents can appropriately grieve.[9] Others think open adoption is not a viable alternative because, too often, adoptive parents or birth parents do not live up to their contract. Either party may cut off contact or may be erratic in following through on the original agreement. Because of these circumstances, a few reformers are calling for the banishment of adoption.[10] In its place they advocate legal guardianship, whereby birth parents would remain in regular contact and would remain the child's parents and legal guardians, bolstered by legal rights that foster parents lack, would provide care and financial support for the child. Are these reforms appropriate steps to take? What problems do they solve or prevent and what other problems might they create? Whose needs do they best meet, and how are the needs of all parties to be prioritized when they conflict?

RETHINKING THE PERFECT SOLUTION

We can see that over the course of history societies have attempted to provide for dependent children according to the existing level of understanding of children's and families' needs. The confidential adoptions that emerged and have been practiced for many years are now under scrutiny.

It has become apparent that the adoptive family system is created out of compelling needs reflecting profound losses affecting each member of the adoption circle. While some fertile parents adopt by preference, most adoptive parents must give up the expectation and rewards of bearing their own biological child. Relinquishing birth parents lose the child they have borne. Adopted children lose the connection to their birth parents. All members of the adoptive family system are defined by their "differentness." The "perfect solution" is rarely anyone's first choice.

While adoption meets real needs, it simultaneously denies deeply held wishes. Adoptive parents wish they could have borne the children they are raising. Children wish that the parents who bore and who raise them could be one and the same. Birth parents wish the circumstances might have been such that they could have raised the child they bore. These wishes were apparent in our earlier snapshots. We saw a birth mother who wished and searched for her son for 28 years after relinquishment, a 13-year-old who wished his birth mother would want him, and an adoptive mother who wished she could have been pregnant with her children. Each member has his or her own grief and pain. In gratitude for needs that are met, unrealized wishes tend to go underground. Thus, the grief and pain that are an inevitable part of the "perfect solution" can remain quite secret and hidden from understanding, with significant consequences for individual and family development. A birth mother finds herself often feeling sad despite fortunate circumstances; she cannot understand why she feels this way. An adoptive mother wonders if she is crazy for still wishing for a pregnancy. A 13-year-old boy finds himself shoplifting, an act that is uncharacteristic for him.

As we have seen, there are many opinions regarding the ways that the difficulties of members of the adoption circle can be remediated or, even better, prevented. To make any sense of this passionate debate, it is necessary to inform ourselves of the many intricate pieces that form the adoption picture.

We need to look at the experiences of birth parents, including the circumstances surrounding the occurrence of an unplanned pregnancy, the decision to relinquish the child, the arrangement made, the separation and ongoing life experiences related to the relinquishment. As we observe these experiences, we can better understand how birth parents attempt to master the developmental tasks of accepting responsibility for the pregnancy, dealing with their feelings toward the fetus and the separation through birth, assessing their competence to parent compared to that of adopting parents, managing the relinquishment, and then mourning their loss over time.

We need to examine the lives of adoptive parents to understand the processes that lead to the decision to adopt, the attachments they make with their children, and the thoughts, feelings, and behaviors that follow. Here we will learn about the tasks of infertile parents in differentiating between reproduction, sexual adequacy, and competency to parent as well as in mourning the loss of the opportunity to bear a biological child. Infertile and preferential adopters alike go on to the tasks of accepting psychological (vs. biological) parenthood, emotionally claiming the child, realigning family relationships to include a nonbiological child, disclosing the adoption, and dealing with the ramifications of genealogical discontinuity in the life of both the child and the family.

We need to study the inner lives of adoptees to understand more about how they experience the move from birth parent to adoptive parent and how they navigate the developmental course when it is complicated by adoption issues. Adoptees' special tasks include recovering from the loss of birth parents, attaching to adopting parents, recognizing the existence of two sets of parents and the resulting ambivalence, and ultimately achieving an integrated identity.

In addition to the individual developmental courses of birth parents, adoptive parents, and adoptees, we need to look at the ways in which members of the adoption circle share common themes. Each member deals with loss, with attachment and separation, and with issues of identity that are adoption-related.

This book is an effort to bring the pieces of a complicated puzzle together in a systematic way. It is written from a lifelong developmental perspective and includes within its purview all members of the adoptive family system. It examines the developmental course of birth parents, adoptive parents, and adoptees and the ways in which their existences interact and impact upon each other over the course of their lifetimes.

Members of the adoption circle will recognize themselves as they read the chapters concerning their developmental tasks and the range of their responses and behaviors, whose descriptions may help bring into focus issues that may have remained illusive. Reading about other members of the circle may enhance both understanding and empathy for their tasks. It is hoped that this added insight will contribute to the ability to acknowledge, cope with, and master the tasks necessary for the development of a normal adoptive family system.

Therapists, child welfare workers, adoption facilitators, and legislators will expand their knowledge of issues relating to the lifelong experiences of birth parents, adoptive parents, and adoptees. They will recognize that the struggle to master special tasks is a necessary and normal part of life in the adoption circle and that clinical, social, and legal interventions must be designed to support these efforts toward mastery.

On the basis of knowledge of the adoption literature and 30 years of personal and professional experience in the adoption circle, I have concluded that the social institution of adoption is still a fine solution to a range of problems. However, to be successful, adoption must be administered and undertaken realistically. This reality must include acknowledgment of the ways in which it is at once similar to and profoundly different from the nonadoptive experience. The adoptive family is similar to all other families since it attempts to provide for the needs of parents and growing children. But it is dissimilar in that it is based on paradoxical relationships: birth parents are at once birth parents but not rearing parents; adoptive parents are rearing parents but not birth parents; adoptees are their adoptive parents' children but not their birth children, their birth parents' progeny but not their children by rearing. Every member of the adoption circle must acknowledge, confront, and master these paradoxes.

To be successful, the experience of adoption must also be undertaken and administered with an understanding of the range of individual and family differences. There is no such thing as ''the adoptee experience,'' ''the birth parent experience,'' or ''the adoptive parent experience.'' While there are commonalities in the issues and developmental tasks to be mastered, each person and each family experiences and deals with these tasks in a unique way. Some family members will experience more success and gratification than others, as is true in biological families. The measure of success is in the ability to master the necessary tasks and achieve a family that meets its members' needs more fully than the real alternatives. Adoption circle members can take satisfaction in the achievement of meeting this significant life challenge.

Let us turn now to look at the life course of each participant in this alternative family system.

CHAPTER 2

TO HAVE BUT NOT
TO HOLD

Developmental Tasks of Birth Parents

HISTORICALLY, BIRTH PARENTS HAVE BEEN the unseen, unheard members of the adoption circle. Until recently, popular and professional literature dealt with them as transitional figures who were only marginally involved in the adoption process despite the fact that they are its initiators. Birth fathers—referred to as "alleged" or "putative"—were barely even mentioned. One author describes the enigma of birth parents who remain parents with no parental functions for their offspring.[1] They sign the papers of relinquishment but do not necessarily sign away parental feelings and concerns. Only recently have the feelings and experiences of these parents been considered in a thoughtful and compassionate manner.[2]

Who becomes a birth parent and what are their experiences? Every year many couples—married and unmarried—conceive babies they have not planned. Some unknown percentage of these couples decide to abort the fetus. Of those who decide to carry the pregnancy to term, most married couples keep and raise their babies. Some unmarried couples also keep their babies while others decide to make an adoption plan for them. The statistics for such decisions are unreliable since there is no national data collection system. In 1982 one researcher conservatively estimated that 549,000 children were placed for adoption by women between the ages of 15 and 44; of these women 88% were unmarried.[3] The numbers that are registered for United States teenagers suggest that unwed pregnancies have risen from 5% in 1960 to 24% in 1976.[4] In the 1970s unmarried nonwhite adolescents' birthrate was two to six times that of white adolescents, but placement of babies was significantly greater in the white population.[5]

The Federal Centers for Disease Control reports that in 1988, the latest year for such statistics, 1,005,299 babies (26% of all newborns) were born to unmarried mothers, most of whom were 20 or older. The ratio of babies kept to those placed for adoption has shifted dramatically: 80% of unmarried mothers placed their babies in 1970, compared to 4% in 1983.[6] In 1986 the National Committee for Adoption reported that there were 51,157 domestic unrelated adoptions and 10,019 foreign adoptions by Americans; about half of these children were infants. The available data, however, is based primarily on agency adoptions and most likely significantly underestimates the number of children relinquished.

Despite the lack of accurate statistics, we can see that there are clear shifts in relinquishment patterns. These shifts reflect the sexual revolution and new freedoms advocated in the 1960s, which culminated in increased social acceptance of out-of-wedlock sexual activity and the babies that resulted.

Some researchers have compared unwed mothers who kept their babies with those who made an adoption plan. One national survey conducted in 1982 found that pregnant women who made an adoption plan for their babies were demographically more similar to women who married before the birth or who had an abortion than they were to unwed mothers who kept their babies.[7] That is, they were more likely to be independent of welfare assistance and more likely to have completed high school than women who decided to keep their babies. In one study mothers who relinquished their babies scored higher on standardized personality tests than did those who kept their babies and thus were considered healthier and "higher functioning."[8] Nevertheless, with current reporting practices, it is impossible to arrive at any accurate demographic profile of a relinquishing parent.

While some pregnancies may result from inadequate birth control devices or from rape, a common experience of relinquishing parents is a failure to manage birth control effectively. There are many theories offered to explain such mismanagement, and these theories recognize a wide range of dynamics, from impulsive, need-satisfying behavior that secondarily produces a pregnancy to sexual behavior that is a culmination of a deep psychological need for a pregnancy or a baby itself. But these dynamics can be true in any couple—married or not, relinquishing or not; what differentiates relinquishing parents is that, for some reason, they decide that they are unwilling or unable to raise their child now.

Many birth mothers, in retrospect, cite simple immaturity as the reason for the pregnancy and lack of resources as the reason for relinquishment. They see themselves as having been typical adolescents who could not believe they would "get into trouble." (We regularly see surveys indicating that a very high percentage of teenagers practice unprotected sex.) Many of these women had wanted to keep their babies but were unable to muster the kind of social and financial support needed to do so. Now, years later, some express bitter resentment at having had to part with their child because of this lack of support. Other birth mothers, however, feel committed to the relinquishment as a decision in everyone's best interests.

Prior to the sexual revolution of the 1960s premarital sex and the babies that resulted were generally considered shameful and unwed parents tended to be "understood" in a variety of negative ways. They were seen as victims of social and economic deprivation, subscribers to lower-class mores and values, and/or psychologically disturbed, as evidenced by the "acting out" that produced the pregnancy. The solution to the problem, relinquishment of the child for adoption (usually referred to as "given away" or "put up for adoption"), was the necessary consequence and was perhaps often seen as a just punishment. Most birth mothers felt they had no options besides a "shotgun wedding" or the stigma of raising the child as an unmarried mother branded with a "scarlet letter." Professionals attempted to support relinquishing mothers by trying to make the experience clean and simple. Homes for unwed mothers and hospital staff discouraged women from even viewing their babies after delivery. The prevailing attitude was that couples (mostly "girls") had gotten "into trouble" by having an unplanned child and were gotten "out of trouble" through the adoption. Thus, the whole problem was thought to be over and solved with the relinquishment. Social service agencies tended to be impatient with the few women who requested more time beyond the legal minimum to make their decision about relinquishment since it seemed so clearly to be the perfect solution.

But times have changed. New social attitudes toward premarital sex have made birth parenthood a speakable and perhaps even intriguing topic. A best-selling novel entitled *Blessings* by Belva Plain sensitively portrays the struggle and anguish of a birth parenting couple,[9] and Lincoln Caplan's *An Open Adoption* was of sufficient popular interest to be excerpted in the *New Yorker*.[10] The increasing prevalence of single parenthood has offered underprepared parents new options.

Researchers in every study completed on birth parents who relinquish are quick to note the highly selective nature of their samples. Respondents are derived primarily from the self-selected group of birth parents who have sought support through national birth parent groups or from clinical samples who have sought psychotherapeutic help. Birth parents have become increasingly active in advocating for themselves and describing their own experiences. We are thus able to glean information from the memoirs and thoughts of relinquishers themselves. We do not know much about those in the birth parent groups who refused to participate in the studies or those who have not attached themselves to support groups or to researched psychotherapy. Thus, what we have heard about birth parents comes from observations by friends, family, or professionals who have had contact with them. While the data are not scientifically rigorous, at least we are beginning to attend to the thoughts and feelings of these previously unseen and unheard members of the adoption circle. We now have some clues about the kinds of processes and tasks with which these people—who are parents and yet not parents—struggle. Our information has been gathered primarily on birth mothers rather than birth fathers, and therefore our discussion will focus more on the women's experiences.

PHASE 1: REACHING THE DECISION TO RELINQUISH

Information about relinquishing parents suggests a wide range of conscious and unconscious factors contributing to the occurrence of the pregnancy. There may be motivational factors such as using pregnancy to hold on to a mate or to get out of the parents' home. There may be a repetition of some family pattern, a living out of a wish to have someone of one's own or to prove one's sexuality. There may be difficulties with procuring and using birth control, particularly among adolescents whose ability to envision consequences may be immature and inadequate. There may be a date rape or stranger rape. There may be genuinely ineffective birth control since no method, besides abstinence, is 100% effective.

Sometimes people find that their conscious or unconscious plans have not produced the expected results, and they feel unready or ill-equipped to proceed with parenting on their own. The unconsciously motivated and genuinely accidental parents-to-be will find themselves in a state of shock, a condition most human beings manage with denial. The need to deny tends to postpone acknowledgment of the pregnancy. Thoughts such as "My/her period is just late" or "The baby has probably already miscarried" or "You can't get pregnant the first time you have sex" can go on for months and can make the choice of abortion impossible. Families can also participate in the denial and not notice such clues as morning sickness or bulky sweatshirts in the summertime.

When the denial is finally undermined, an acknowledgment of the pregnancy occurs. Each woman decides whether or not to inform and include the biological father in her planning. Sometimes the decision may be unambivalent since there may be a strong reason not to want to include him. The circumstances behind this unequivocal decision are highly varied. One extreme may be rape or date rape, where no further contact with the father is preferable to any amount of financial or other support. A woman may feel just as certain about not wanting to involve a man she loves for fear of extracting a premature commitment or other guilt-induced behavior. "Perhaps I wasn't fair," reflected Anna B.,

> but I wanted our relationship to develop naturally, just between the two of us. I felt there was no way that could happen either if we married to keep the baby or if we, together, relinquished it. It would inevitably muddy the waters. So I took responsibility for the decision and went away to give birth. We resumed our relationship for another year or so and then drifted apart. I feel satisfied that the relationship took its own course. And I never told him.

Other women in ongoing or short-lived relationships press for the biological father to meet his share of the responsibility with more or less success. Nowadays, identifying biological fathers has legal ramifications; some women may choose to register the father as unknown rather than contend with his or his family's claim to the child.

The individual woman or the couple also makes a decision about who else to include in their planning and their efforts to muster necessary resources. Some turn to the woman's family only, some to the man's family only, some to both, and some to neither. Variables include the nature of existing relationships with their families, imagined attitudes of the families toward an unplanned pregnancy, and the potential of support toward an acceptable resolution. Some individuals or couples will decide not to inform parents, feeling that it would cause unnecessary and irredeemable pain. One young woman floated a trial balloon with her mother, telling her about an unmarried "friend" who had become pregnant. Her mother's response made it clear that she felt the pregnancy reflected a total failure of the family and all the values it had attempted to represent for generations. Though the young women did not agree with this assessment, she decided not to subject her widowed mother to such devastating thoughts and not to subject herself to the consequences. Other women fear that parents would become punitive rather than helpful. Susan T., who, like many others, turned instead to friends and other family members, said:

> I came from a strict religious family that has little tolerance for straying from the established moral laws, judging from my growing up years and watching how they responded to others who didn't measure up in some way. I think they would see this pregnancy—whether I abort or relinquish—as absolutely unforgivable. In one way or another, I would become persona non grata and would never be allowed to live this down. I see no reason to do this to myself.

Popular culture is replete with the "Mom, I'm pregnant" scene or the girl with a baby in her arms on the doorstep. These scenes can be highly dramatic, with intense expression of feelings of all sorts. Parental anger can culminate in temporary or permanent disowning and family schism. It is also possible that irrevocable bonds can be forged when family members embrace each other in the depths of despair: "I never knew if they would really be there for me if I disappointed them. It has made a huge difference to me to find that they were." Some families may just get through the experience by harboring resentments that periodically reemerge over time.

When parents or other family members are informed of the pregnancy, it becomes necessary for the birth parents to deal with *their* thoughts and feelings. Some birth parents and their families dismiss the option of abortion immediately for religious, health, financial, or other reasons and never reconsider it. Others struggle with themselves and with each other toward a resolution.

Prior to the *Roe* v. *Wade* decision and the legalization of abortion in 1973, women's options involved applying for a legal therapeutic abortion or undergoing an illegal one. Therapeutic abortions were allowed only when the pregnancy was deemed life-threatening, either medically or because of risk of suicide. Seeking either a therapeutic or illegal abortion was most often a humiliating, painful experience. With legalization and increased social acceptance, abortion has become a safer, psychologically less stressful option. A recent study by Gold-Steinberg comparing legal with illegal abortions notes a shift in the research literature from the 1930s through the 1980s: studies viewed abortion first as a trauma (1935–1951), then as a crisis (1967–1976), then as a stressful situation evoking coping responses (1984–1985), and most recently as a weighing of important relational obligations (1982–1988).[11] Her study notes the trend of women keeping or aborting over relinquishing as more real options have become medically, socially, and legally available to them. Prior to the sexual revolution of the 1960s and the legalization of abortion in the 1970s, many women felt they had no choice but to bear and relinquish their babies. Neither an illegal abortion nor living in shame with a child they were not ready to parent seemed like a viable option.

Today some women who have decided they cannot raise their child still choose relinquishment over abortion. Of these, some feel abortion is morally wrong. Some feel a bond with the fetus even in the earliest months. As one woman said, "I made the mistake; my child shouldn't have to pay for it"; through adoption she felt she could give her child a good life. Some women feel gratified by the belief that they are providing both life for their child and a child for a longing couple.

There is the issue of responsibility for the pregnancy; whose "fault" was it—his, hers, both, or no one's? This is a time when blame is likely to be lobbed about for failures past and present. Allied with ascribed or assumed responsibility is guilt and shame. Sally P., 17, discussing her pregnancy with a social worker who had worked with her family, was full of anxiety and rage: she blamed her mother for not teaching her about birth control and her date for pressuring her into "going all the way." Her judgment about planning for the baby was clouded by her determination to punish those she saw at fault. With help, Sally was able to acknowledge her disappointments in others as well as her disappointment in herself. In so doing, she was able to go on to make a decision she felt was in her baby's best interest. Many young people, like Sally, need to accept responsibility for their own contribution and to work through their blame and anger for the other's responsibility until they reach a point of relief, if not yet forgiveness; there must be sufficient resolution to allow for progress toward seeking proper medical care and planning for the future of the child.

In the course of planning, there is likely to be internal and external conflict. Both parents struggle with their own conflicting feelings about the child: they may simultaneously want it and not want it; they may both love it and hate it for complicating their lives. The mother and father fight with themselves, with each other, and often with family and other interested parties in attempting to make a decision.

If the balance turns toward placement birth mothers may rely on the belief that they are being good parents by doing what is in the best interests of the child. There is comfort in thinking of oneself as similar to the subject of King Solomon who placed her child's welfare above her own. At the same time, they are plagued with the incongruousness of thinking of themselves as loving parents and simultaneously giving a child away. There may be pressure from peers and others who see relinquishment as a selfish act. Despite the supportive insistence by others that relinquishment is best for the child, they may worry that they are really doing what is best for themselves. "My head tells me one thing, but my heart tells me another," laments Mary G.

> I know that I am not ready to take good enough care of this child and that an adoptive family would give him much more emotionally, financially, and culturally. I really believe that. What I also know is that I don't want to take care of him now.

Keeping him would put me on a life course that would be un-
bearable for me. I'm a regular middle-class girl. I want to finish
school, have a career, marry a nice middle-class guy and live an
ordinary life. I couldn't possibly do that if I had a child now. My
heart says I'm being selfish for placing my own life goals over
the hurt feelings of a child who will know I gave him away.

Even when birth parents are able to repress these feelings and act
on the relinquishment, these conflicts are likely to be stirred up
and revisited over time.

PHASE 2: PREPARATION FOR RELINQUISHMENT

Relinquishing parents have many decisions to make in arranging
for the placement of their child. They must decide whether they
will plan through an established agency or through a private facilitator. This decision is based on their access to varying resources
and their own particular needs for financial, medical, and social
services. Women sometimes live in homes for unwed mothers or
privately arranged housing. Since the mid-1980s, with increased
openness in adoption practices, relinquishing parents have had
to make additional decisions regarding the type of contract they
wish to establish with adopting parents. They need to decide how
active they wish to be in choosing the parents rather than have
the agency or facilitator choose. They need to decide how much
and what kind of contact (if any) they want to continue to have
after the placement is made. They may feel pressured by the
agency or facilitator toward a particular contract based on the
agent's ideology or the wishes of potential adopting parents.

The decision to place the baby for adoption does not in itself
achieve the *emotional* relinquishment of parental rights. This has
its own processes. Mothers have experienced a physical and emotional attachment to the fetus for nine months. Many fathers feel
similar connections. The process of separation through birth is
a well-recognized shift for all mothers, commonly precipitating
postpartum "blues" and, in some cases, actual depression. For
relinquishing parents, the entire pregnancy is fraught with issues
of attachment and loss. At one extreme, some mothers decide to
enjoy the attachment until the baby is gone; they live for today,
nurturing the pregnancy and the baby in whatever ways they can
while they have it. At the other extreme are those who try to deny
any emotional attachment in an attempt to protect themselves

from future loss. In between are those who experience attaching and having to let go all at the same time. Each warm moment of response to the moving fetus is followed by another moment of anticipatory grief.

The birth process itself reflects internal and external discomfort and conflict. Rarely do relinquishing parents experience a supportive system around them as they attempt to manage their physical and emotional pain. Vested interests become palpable as child welfare agents and prospective adoptive parents await eagerly in the wings. Hospital staff often function efficiently but without sensitivity to the circumstances. For example, most maternity wards distribute babies for feedings at regularly prescribed times; a relinquishing mother may watch her roommate receive and feed her infant while she observes or feeds a baby she may never see again. Her experience is very different from that of the other new mothers, but she is likely to be treated similarly. Sally B. held her baby immediately following the birth but decided to have no further contact. She describes seeing those babies distributed to their mothers as a "nightmare" and used that time to go to the hospital chapel and cry.

Relinquishing parents frequently report the isolation, loneliness, and sadness they felt during the pregnancy and birth. Sandra F. was a warm, perky 18-year-old who had enjoyed a close relationship with her mother but had decided, because of her mother's religious beliefs, not to inform her of the pregnancy. "I guess I always imagined my mother being there when I had a baby," she said. "Perhaps most women want their mothers around. I felt so lonely without her—I ached to at least call her. It was really depressing to me to go through such an important experience without her."

During pregnancy or after delivery, teenagers may find themselves particularly isolated and estranged from their peers. Sensing or predicting peer disapproval, they may keep their secret, feeling very alone and different. And, in fact, they *are* different in that their preoccupation is with the lost child rather than with the customary interests of teenage life. They have experienced a milestone often far from the social norm, which has probably produced some mixture of sobering, maturity, and trauma that they feel sets them apart.

Satisfaction is derived from the achievement of producing a healthy baby, who then has the best chance for a selected home. When there are handicaps or physical anomalies, issues of guilt and shame reemerge and are intensified. The original placement plan may be canceled through private or public arrangements. Foster or institutional care may now be the available option. The comforting thoughts of one's child living in more fortuitous circumstances are dashed. Like any parent facing placement of a child with special needs, relinquishing parents anguish over the child's potential quality of life compared to what the biological home might have provided. Once again the kind of supports, services, and comforts available to other parents are rarely provided to the relinquishers. With a healthy child or not, they tend to be left on their own to deal with issues surrounding the birth.

Complicating birth parents' internal and relationship conflicts regarding the act of relinquishment are the social attitudes and pressures exerted upon them. Some family members, friends, and others will support the decision to relinquish as best for the child, mother, and/or the couple. Others may oppose it on different grounds. Some may see it as too grave a loss, one that will produce a lifetime of sadness and regret. Others may make moralistic judgments against it: "How can you give away your own child? It is unnatural, inhuman, and not God's will." There may be vested interests in wanting additional family members to carry on the family name and genealogy. All of these needs, wishes, and judgments exacerbate the couple's ambivalence and may make it even more difficult for them to determine where the balance lies for them. "My mother convinced me that keeping the baby would ruin my life," Judy J. reflected. "I now think she was saying that my keeping the baby would have ruined *her* life. I wish I had not let her impose her needs on me. I never really made the decision for myself."

Along with the relinquishment comes everyone else's thoughts and feelings. Grandparents grieve for their (perhaps first) grandchild. As they stand by their son or daughter and this decision, they, too, say good-bye to that infant. They may grieve both for themselves and for their child. They, too, will remember forever. Siblings—the baby's aunts and uncles—similarly experience a loss and sometimes exert pressure to keep the baby themselves. Birth parents often also rely on the judgment of experts in the field who believe that adoption is best for everyone. Thus, personal and professional pressures can have an impact on the mother's ambivalences in a way that encourages her to deny her own wishes and needs.

In order to conclude that relinquishment serves the best interests of the child, birth parents must believe one of the basic tenets of the adoption system: adoptive parents are better able to provide for the child and therefore are more competent. Maintaining that belief tempers their anxiety about the self-interested quality of the decision and contributes to greater peace. However, everyone has heard of or read of incompetent or even abusive adoptive parents. Birth parents take a risk in the relinquishment. They hope that agency home studies are valid or that private matchmakers are acting competently and in good faith. Even when birth parents participate in the selection of adoptive parents, they can only hope that their intuitions and judgments have been good ones. For the sake of their emotional well-being and the ability to go ahead with the relinquishment, they cannot afford to dwell on lurking concerns regarding the quality of the adoptive homes and must repress images of any less-than-ideal circumstances. With increasing involvement of birth parents in the choice of adoptive parents, there have been instances of choosing and "unchoosing" potential parents when birth parents became aware of what might have been relatively minor lifestyle issues that did not fit the idealized image of upbringing they held for their child. Jane, a mature, sophisticated woman in her early thirties who had majored in early childhood education, rejected one family after another as she judged them inadequate for the raising of her child. Finally, recognizing her need to find the nonexistent perfect home—one better than she herself could offer—she turned the selection over to an adoption agency.

At the same time that they consider relinquishment, birth parents assess their own abilities and capacities. It *is* possible to raise an unplanned child successfully, and birth parents may know people who did so. On the other hand, birth parents may also know of cases where the results were disastrous. They may wonder where they would fall on this continuum and may ask themselves, if I really tried, if I am willing to sacrifice or postpone some goals and wishes, would the outcome be better than adoption?

Important issues that affect the ambivalence have to do with the birth parents' own family and life experience. The quality of home life sought for their child is likely to reflect a comparison with their experience with their own parents. If they were raised in poverty, for example, the idea of their child having opportunities they did not have may be a very convincing element in the decision to relinquish. If they were raised by a struggling single parent, the idea of providing a two-parent family may clearly determine the decision.

Similarly, there are important psychological issues related to the birth parents' experiences of separation and abandonment. If one has suffered with such feelings in the past, it may feel totally unacceptable to place one's own child in such circumstances. "I was abandoned by my father when I was three," said Tony F. "The hurt and resentment has stayed with me for a lifetime. I would never make my child go through that. I will do anything to keep him." Others who have experienced a safe and secure upbringing may minimize the effects of relinquishment and feel that the opportunities in the adoptive family will far outweigh the possible psychological damages of the relinquishment. The latter position is the one that has historically been taken by adoption agencies. The increasing literature describing the additional tasks of adopted people may be discomforting to birth parents and may make their decision even more difficult.

There are a number of conclusions birth mothers can come to in support of the decision to relinquish their baby. They can conclude that it is impossible for them under any circumstances to provide care that equals that of an adoptive home. This conclusion subsumes the belief that the child's feelings about having been relinquished will be outweighed by his positive family experience. Another possible conclusion for birth mothers is that while they would be able to provide as well as adoptive parents, they are unwilling to make the necessary sacrifices and therefore see adoption as an acceptable alternative. A third possible conclusion is that they would be able to care for their child adequately only if circumstances were different (for example, if they had completed their education and had a job and financial security) and since they do not have these circumstances, they cannot accept the responsibility. Birth mothers process many thoughts and feelings in drawing conclusions and making their decisions. Social norms, their own life experiences, current resources, and future goals are all weighed against the potential adoptive home. The balance of weight toward relinquishment may be overwhelming for some and only slight for others. Whatever the balance, anxiety about comparative competencies may not be laid to rest.

This phase of preparation for relinquishment is fraught, for most, with many mixed and conflicting thoughts and feelings. Roberta L. was distressed by the pushes and pulls she felt in so many different directions. She felt attached to her baby but did not want to raise it. She wanted to satisfy her mother's wish to keep the baby in the family but did not want that complication in her life. She wondered if she would ever feel fully confident that her child was being cared for properly by adoptive parents. After months of confusion and distress, Roberta came to see that her circumstance was inherently conflictual and that the answers would never emerge as pure and simple. She would make her decision on the balance of what she felt was right for her and her baby and accepted that she would continue to struggle with her remaining mixed feelings over time. Mastery at this stage thus required an acceptance of ambivalent feelings. This acceptance allowed Roberta to go on to make reasonable decisions for herself and her child without denying any of her feelings. She was gratified at this achievement since a few years earlier she had watched a close friend become paralyzed by indecision. The friend's baby, who remained in foster care while the family stayed mired in controversy, endured three shifts of care before being permanently placed in an adoptive home at age 2½. Roberta was pleased to be able to provide a permanent home for her baby shortly after birth.

PHASE 3: THE RELINQUISHMENT

The actual placement of the child requires birth parents to confront the physical and emotional loss of their offspring. While some process of grieving and letting go may have occurred in the course of the pregnancy, the physical separation is a further precipitant. Each person mourns in his or her own way, and relinquishing parents must deal with some issues that are different from the issues of parents who have lost a child in other ways, such as through permanent institutionalization or death. In previous decades physical separation often coincided with the birth itself since relinquishing parents were discouraged from ever seeing or holding their child. Nowadays it is more common for there to be some physical contact, and in some cases infants may even be breast-fed for a period of time. In addition to physical contact between birth parent and infant, we are hearing more and more about immediate (delivery room) contact between adoptive parents and infants. In *An Open Adoption* Lincoln Caplan describes a situation in which the birth mother insisted that the infant be placed in the arms of the awaiting adoptive mother immediately following birth so that he could bond with her scent and body, a choice that placed the needs of the child above her own wishes.[12]

Whatever the circumstances or practice, at birth the process of attachment that has existed throughout the pregnancy is now fraught with loss. Even in an active, open adoption, the child will never again belong to the birth mother in the same way. She will never experience the dailiness of parenting this child—the bedtime stories, the runny noses, the kissed scraped knees, the temper tantrums, the "I did it myself," or the "Mom, I'm home." Visiting with the child and/or hearing about the child's progress is not the same as living through the pleasures and the pain. While there are some groups and agencies committed to assisting birth parents through this ordeal, our social structure as a whole offers no rites, ceremonies, or customs that validate the loss and offer support to the grieving mother. Friends and family may or may not be able to empathize with and acknowledge the pain. People who try to comfort often do so by reminding the mother that it is "all for the best." Once again, the belief in the "perfect solution" may undermine the realities of the personal pain involved and contribute to keeping this pain secret and insidious. Acknowledgment of the loss by the couple and by others who are involved makes it possible to more adequately cope with its pain. Toward this goal, some agencies and practitioners now encourage the enactment of a formal ceremony where birth parents say good-bye to their child and bestow on adoptive parents the responsibility for its love and care. In return, adoptive parents take the child into their arms and promise their devotion. Each birth mother needs to find her own way of saying good-bye. Some may find the public ceremony most useful; others may prefer a private moment or a ceremony of their own. Whatever the form, there needs to be an acknowledgment of this biological bond and of the separation in order to effectively move on to further tasks.

There is a study of the mourning process in relinquishing mothers, based on interviews with 22 women in psychotherapy, entitled "Solomon's Mothers: A Special Case of Pathological Bereavement."[13] In addition to describing these women and the ways bereavement can be pathological, this study may help us understand more about this special case of bereavement, what elements might be unique to relinquishing mothers, and how they might achieve their own specific form of nonpathological grieving.

The authors describe the six stages of grieving that are commonly delineated for relinquishing women in the literature: (1) the process of realization, (2) an alarm reaction, (3) an urge to search for and find the lost child in form, (4) anger and guilt, (5) feelings of internal loss of self or mutilation, and (6) identification phenomena.

1. The Process of Realization.   The most common human response to loss is denial: "I can't (won't) believe it." When someone dies, survivors, despite their pain, often go on about daily life and customary pursuits as a way of denying the unavoidable impact of the loss on their lives and well-being. It takes many different forms of confrontation with reality to move toward the necessary realistic acknowledgment and acceptance of the loss. Only then can their lives be reorganized without the lost person and resumed with only the memories. This process is more complicated for relinquishing parents because the child, though no longer physically present, still exists. There is no funeral, no cremation or burial, no recognized statement of finality from which one ultimately accepts the reality that there is no way of reconstituting the lost loved one. Relinquishing parents' fantasies of reunion are bolstered by the reality of the child's continued existence. It is therefore necessary to achieve acceptance of a different kind of loss—that is, loss of one's child in a permanent, everyday way—even when there is an open adoption. On the way to the acceptance, relinquishing parents may experience attitudes from "It's the same as if she were dead" to "He's still mine and I'll get him back one day." They struggle to accept the enigmatic state of having given birth to a child they may continue to care about and yet have given away. Even in those open adoptions where there is regular visiting and actual child care given, the child is not theirs to have and to hold as he or she is to others.

2. Alarm Reaction.   This phase represents the experience of shattered security when familiar and predictable beliefs and behaviors seem obsolete. Excluding those who choose to become surrogate mothers, it would be rare for anyone to expect or plan to one day bear and then relinquish a child. Panicky, alarmed responses and thoughts of "How could this have happened?" and "How could I have done this?" are understandable, even in those circumstances where birth parents solidly believed relinquishment was the best thing to do. "I never imagined it would feel this way—as if a part of me has died. In some ways it feels like a stillbirth—only worse—because I *let* him leave me. I've done this to myself as well as to him." There are likely to be excruciating moments of existential concerns: "What does this mean about me—what have I done to him?" Sometimes a response to "What have I done?" is to entertain fantasies of undoing the harm by searching for and retrieving the child.

3. *Searching.* People grieving over the death of a loved one frequently report a preconscious kind of searching for the lost person. There are moments of feeling certain of seeing the lost one's face in a crowd or hearing familiar footsteps on the stairs. The bereaved may themselves take on characteristics of the lost person in the way they dress, behave, think, or feel as a way of keeping the deceased close and present. Usually, in time, these experiences diminish. For relinquishing parents, again, there is a difference. The lost child may, in fact, be seen. He may be seen in fantasy, by accident, or by plan (as in an open adoption). Many such parents report a lifelong preconscious search, being always on the lookout for a person of the correct age, gender, and physical characteristics. The urgency may quicken with time with the hope that the child has become old enough to begin searching for his or her birth parents; the fact that the child has reached 18 or 21 may intensify birth parents' hopes. The urge to search, to have and to hold again, can be reinforced by reality and is unlikely to diminish easily over time, as most often happens following a death.

4. *Anger and Guilt.* When something bad happens, it is human nature to hold someone responsible, either the self or others. Thus, it is common for there to be a struggle between guilt and blame. In ordinary grieving, people frequently blame themselves for somehow contributing to the death or for having failed the lost person in some other way. They may concomitantly blame others, such as caretakers, doctors, or cigarette companies. Over time, they tend to sort out legitimate blame from the reality of life, which includes the knowledge that a death is not necessarily anyone's fault. Relinquishing parents must confront their own responsibility, for they created the circumstances of their own loss. This is frequently reinforced by others who implicitly express the judgment: "You made your own problems, so you cannot complain." What the birth parents are struggling with at this point is responsibility for the relinquishment, rather than for the pregnancy. They may not feel fully responsible for the decision to make an adoption plan. Blame may be felt toward friends, fam-

ily, and child welfare personnel who they feel pressured them toward their decision or withheld a kind of support that might have made other options possible. The "Solomon's Mothers" study found that anger at third parties intensified rather than diminished over time. We do not know how common this phenomenon is for relinquishing mothers. It may be a defense against their own self-blame, or it may be an accurate assessment of their circumstances. Still, we would expect that all birth parents would need to deal with issues of guilt and blame at the time of relinquishment and perhaps forever after.

5. *Feelings of Loss of Self.*   When people deal with a loss, there is commonly an experience of losing the sense of themselves as they were prior to the loss. They may feel they have "gone to pieces" and must now reconstruct themselves without that person in their lives. One would expect this process to be intensified for relinquishing mothers who have reported the feeling that their baby was ripped away from them. Their bodies may feel empty and shattered; some may even feel permanently damaged and incapable of ever bearing a child normally. Stacy P. grew up in a midwestern family she classified as "normal." As far as she knew, nothing unusual or "abnormal" had ever happened through the last several generations. Life was orderly and predictable. Family members did what needed to be done and enjoyed life's pleasures in what seemed an uncomplicated manner. For Stacy, the relinquishment of her baby felt bizarre. She had nightmares of being a figure in a science fiction scenario, giving birth in an unnatural way. She felt like a pariah, like one who was strange and hurtful compared to others in her family. Meeting other women in similar circumstances provided some temporary relief, but Stacy never stopped feeling like the "weird one" in her family.

Men also report an encroachment on their sense of themselves through the loss, but it is experienced more in relational terms than in the kind of physical experiences women describe. Men describe a compromise in their sense of themselves as protectors and providers. Robert J., who came from a large family in which he had taken care of many younger siblings, said, "I would never have believed that I would turn my own child over to someone else's care. I think it was the best thing to do under the circumstances, but I felt like it just wasn't me to do such a thing." Overcoming the guilt may take many healing experiences over many years.

6. Identification Phenomena. One way of keeping the lost person is to become like him or her in some way. Commonly, there is a period of what mental health professionals call "identification with the lost object." It can take the form of experiencing the lost person's symptoms or of taking on aspects of is or her appearance or behavior. As the emotional "letting go" takes place, there is usually a natural diminution of this behavior and one resumes an identity apart from the lost person. For the relinquishing mother this "letting go" means giving up her sense of herself as being attached to the child in a direct, maternal way. She may at first maintain the experience of the pregnancy or early contact with the child. She herself may feel like an abandoned child longing for the mother she imagines her child missing. Fathers, too, may express feeling "lost" as they feel their child is lost. They may feel displaced and disoriented, finding themselves unable to "settle" for some period of time. They may struggle with the question "Who am I if I am not a protector and a providing father?"

The good birth parent does everything within his or her power to produce a healthy baby and to arrange for the best possible home and developmental experience. Having done this, one can take pride in one's birth parent identity while at the same time regretting the inability to be an upbringing parent. The task then, is to accept one's birth parenthood but give up one's identity as an upbringing parent. This is not an easy task.

The authors of "Solomon's Mothers" note a number of factors that delayed or suppressed the grief process in their clinical sample: (1) the loss may have been socially stigmatized, (2) external events may have prevented the expression of feelings of loss, (3) there may have been uncertainty as to whether or not there was an actual loss, (4) there may have been an absence of mourning at the normal and expected time, and (5) mourning rituals were often lacking. We see evidence of these factors—the poignant reports of the loneliness, the isolation, the not knowing what to do or where to turn—in every memoir and every case report.

Birth parents can develop their own ways of mourning effectively. Rose T. describes how she secretly gave herself the same time and space she had observed in her family's Jewish tradition of mourning. She stayed home for seven days, doing little else but thinking about her relinquished son. She said good-bye to him in many ways. Over time, her grief began to give way to thoughts of him in his happy adoptive home. She planned to light candles for him on his birthday each year and make wishes for him. Other birth parents invent their own secret rituals marking the birthday, the relinquishment day, or other moments that are significant to them. Some maintain contact with professionals or agencies who were involved with the birth experience and confirm and validate their feelings in this way. Birth parent groups enable members to provide support for each other. In these ways, relinquishing parents deal with this phase of grief and go on.

PHASE 4: POST-RELINQUISHMENT STAGE (MIDDLE YEARS)

The completion of the events and procedures of adoption free relinquishing parents to resume their customary pursuits. They are expected to return to work or school and to pick up where they left off. However, the emotional issues do not cease and sometimes interfere with resuming normal life.

The mourning process continues far beyond the adoption, that is, throughout the lifetime in different ways and with varying intensity. Relinquishing parents report a kind of fantasized tracking they do of their child, imagining him or her both in daily life and at developmental milestones. "I never know what will trigger an association to my child," reported Jessica M., 10 years after the relinquishment of her daughter.

> I find myself with feelings I don't understand and then have to figure out what precipitated them. Over these many years, I've come to see that there is some association to Janey (the name I gave her). For example, I remember vividly five years ago arriving at work on a fall day extremely anxious and depressed. I went to the rest room and sobbed, with no idea why I was feeling this way. I had felt fine when I left the house. I really thought I must be having a nervous breakdown. I later recalled having driven by the local elementary school—it was the first day after summer vacation. It would have been Janey's very first day of school. I was devastated at not being there with her and anxious about how she was. I had never been a good student myself and fear that she is also having difficulty and is unhappy in school. There are other times when I have unexpected feelings of satisfaction. When I was out to dinner recently, I found myself feeling especially good—again, for no reason I could

identify. It had been a family restaurant and I observed many seemingly happy families enjoying themselves. I come from a poor, unhappy family, one that would never have been in this scene. I imagined Janey being there with her adoptive family and felt happy that I had enabled her to have pleasures and opportunities I didn't have.

Birthdays can be particularly mournful or bittersweet as parents imagine their child in good circumstances but far away. This is a time when they might wonder if the child is thinking of them and what kind of feelings they may have about the relinquishment. "It used to be that I went into a deep funk around Christmas every year," Kathy O. recalled.

> I began to think that it had to do with the holidays and avoided celebrations. I finally figured out that it wasn't "holiday" but "birthday" that was my nemesis. My son was born on December twelfth and I signed the papers on the twenty-third, partially so that he could spend his first Christmas at "home." It was a very blue Christmas that year and every year since. I've done much better since I've figured it out. I just consider December my time to remember him and say good-bye again. I imagine him with his family and his presents and I am happy for him. I hope he is content enough not to be angry at me. I wish he could know that I am thinking of him. Maybe he does.

Both Jessica and Kathy were able to attend to their inexplicable feelings and identify them as adoption related. In so doing they were able to address the salient issues and develop ways of coping with them. They might otherwise have gotten stuck in their confused, unhappy feelings and been unable to move on.

The mourning continues for the stages of childhood unshared. Birth parents imagine a growing child with his or her genes developing in a separate and distant world. Even when there are no second thoughts about the decision to relinquish, there may continue to be a sadness about the child.

Some parents report that not a day goes by that they don't think of their child. Others report the intensity diminishing over time and intensifying only around birthdays, holidays, or other milestones. With the intensification often comes a reemerging wish to search for the child. Concomitantly, birth parents may fear the secret being revealed in both their world and the child's world:

> As much as I long for him and want to see him, I know that bringing him or even the news of him into my life would destroy everything I've worked for these many years. I have a husband and other children now. None of them know. I am convinced that it would destroy my marriage and devastate my children if this child reappeared. I know that some people do have successful reunions. I just don't think it could work for me.

Sometimes birth parents' worst fears about the impact of a reunion are dispelled. This is nicely dramatized in the novel *Blessings* when a child searches out and approaches her birth mother at a particularly inauspicious time in the mother's life, as she was preparing for a marriage.[14] Being convinced that her fiancé would reject her if he knew of the child, the mother tries to fend off the child and then allows unfortunate circumstances to drive away her husband-to-be. In the end, he learns of the child and spontaneously accepts her. This fictional tale dramatizes an event that is often real. Birth parents are sometimes hard on themselves and project a disapproval onto others that does not exist in them. The projection may be an expression of guilt or self-blame that continues to exist but has been covered over as an issue of the past.

Birth parents also express concerns regarding the possible impact of a search on the child:

> If he is happy and healthy and has accepted the relinquishment, I don't want to stir things up for him. God knows, I don't want to make his life any more difficult. I've already complicated it enough. On the other hand, suppose he is unhappy or not well treated and wants to come live with me. Do I want to take on this responsibility now? Do I want to deal with whatever resentment he may have about the original relinquishment?

These ambivalent feelings may preclude active searching behavior and the concern remains forever part of one's fantasy life.

The profound experience of relinquishing a child can have an impact in many areas of ordinary life. Whatever the circumstance, there is a permanent issue with the other birth parent. Couples who were married to each other or remained together following the relinquishment may suffer individual or shared feelings of anguish over the years. There may be continued active or passive blame of one or the other for having had to take that step. "If you were making more money" or "If you hadn't been a drinker" or "If you hadn't insisted on staying in school" may be expressions that are brandished at times when memories of the relinquishment become painful. We know that the chronic illness or death of a child constitutes extreme marital stress and correlates with an extraordinarily high divorce rate. It is possible that the presence of the mate serves as a painful reminder of the illness or loss of the child and there is relief in removing that daily confrontation. There are no known divorce statistics for relinquishing parents, but given the similarity of their issues, it would not be surprising if the figures come close to those for parents whose children were chronically ill or died.

If the father was never informed of his progeny, the birth mother may feel residual guilt around this decision or regret not having shared the event and the responsibility. She may come to feel, even if she had good reasons not to inform him at the time, that a father is entitled to know of the existence of his own child and make his own decision regarding the nature of his responsibility. If he was informed and was unresponsive or disapproving, there may be continued feelings of guilt, disappointment, anger, or revenge. With more maturity, the birth father himself may feel guilt, shame, and regret about his abdication of responsibility both to the birth mother and to their child. He may try to make up for it by a commitment to other people or causes. One man who at 17 fled his girlfriend's pregnancy became a devoted child care worker in a facility for wards of the court. He was unusual in his empathy for the children's feelings of abandonment and was inexhaustible in his activity. Recognizing the driven quality of his work, he entered therapy and came to see that he had been attempting to take care of abandoned children as he had not taken care of his own son. In the process he was able to make amends to his girlfriend and forgive himself sufficiently to embark on a more rational and satisfying life.

For many others the feelings related to the relinquishment have an impact on continued contact with the other parent or even carry over to other relationships. There may be periodic or prolonged inhibition of sexual feelings, which birth parents may feel culminated in so much anguish. They may deprive themselves of sensuous pleasure as punishment for the "bad deed" of relinquishment. There is the suggestion in the literature that relinquishing parents may later have higher than average fertility problems. The studies are not conclusive, since they do not have control groups for age and number of pregnancies, but with what we know about the feelings of many relinquishers, it is entirely possible that there are difficulties with subsequent sexuality and fertility and that these problems are unconscious expressions of guilt and the wish to undo the previous mistake and prevent another.

Studies of these parents also suggest that relationships with their other children (born before or after the relinquished child) may be affected by the relinquishment. What we hear is that they do not take their children for granted and may be more intense and protective in these relationships than other parents. It is as if they give these children what they were unable to give the lost one, as if they are holding on dearly to those they still have. Ironically, this is the very same description we frequently hear of adoptive parents who hold dear and (too?) close the children they are so grateful to have.

In resuming life pursuits, then, it is necessary for relinquishing parents to deal with their continued mourning and to understand and manage the impact the event may have on current relationships. They need to separate the past from the present and recognize regretted acts of the past as ones to learn from. This forgiving of oneself and others allows new relationships and experiences to be unencumbered. Successfully struggling with the tasks of this phase allows for relief and resolution and the move on to later life.

PHASE 5: LATER LIFE

Understandably, we have little information about relinquishing parents in later life. People who would have gone through this experience in more repressed times are likely to continue to be more uncomfortable discussing it publicly even many years later. Our information comes mostly from reports from adult adoptees who have experienced a reunion with birth parents who are in their later years. Most are reported to be quite self-sufficient, with varying degrees of interest in the child. A few, who are lonely and needful, turn to their birth child for care and comfort in their waning years. There are those who feel the reunion completes important unfinished business. One birth mother stated, ''I would never have been able to seek her out myself, but now that she has come to me, I feel I can rest in peace. I am eternally grateful that she searched for me.'' Others are disturbed by disruptions of the equilibrium they established after the relinquishment and don't feel ready or able to deal with the reemergence of the child they said good-bye to so many years before.

Relying on conventional wisdom, we would expect a continued mourning later in life as birth parents strive to accept some final facts, for example, that advancing age means that the time to learn about the whereabouts and welfare of the relinquished child is now or never. A few aging people feel an urgency to act on this realization. More commonly, fantasies of search and/or reunion that were entertained in earlier years are never realized. Thus, there is a final sadness for birth parents in accepting that they will never know or know of their child. Moreover, there is the fact that there may now be grandchildren who are also unknown. The relinquishing parent may never know when he or she passed the milestone of becoming a grandparent. For most relinquishing parents, then, life ends with many questions left unanswered.

An increasing number of birth parents feel that the value of a search far outweighs all other possible negative effects on themselves and their children. They are earnest and single-minded in their efforts. Some relinquishing parents in recent years have become politically active in an effort to make searches possible and to give themselves and future parents the right to information about and contact with their children by birth.

Searches and reunions occur through mutual registries in 35 states and through private investigations and search groups. While there are no available statistics for searches and reunions, this process has become more clearly visible and socially sanctioned. A book entitled *Birthbond*, which describes the aftermath of reunions, was published in 1989.[15] This book offers descriptions of the post-reunion experiences of 30 birth mothers who volunteered to participate in unstructured interviews. Half the reunions were less than three years in duration, and half were between three and ten years. The authors cite age and gender of adoptees, as well as their feelings of belonging in the birth family, as major factors in the relative pain or pleasure for birth mothers in post-reunion experiences. Birth mothers reuniting with teenagers most often described them as troubled whereas older adoptees appeared more stable and in adult transitions such as marriages or childbearing. Gender emerged as a significant factor since some mothers reported a sexual attraction to their sons, which has been called "genetic sexual attraction" by post-reunion observers. Sometimes there was a shared romantic feeling between mother and son, causing each of them discomfort and distress. Several hypotheses to explain this phenomenon are offered. One hypothesis suggests that the feelings are related to a desire for physical bonding since mothers have the wish to hold and fondle their offspring as one does with infants and young children. Thus, motherly desire merges with womanly erotic desire. A second related explanation suggests that the intimacy sought through reunion merges with adult sexual intimacy. A third explanation relates the romantic feeling to the development of a narcissistic mirroring where one falls in love with someone who looks like oneself. The authors report that despite the discomfort these feelings produced, genetic sexual attraction did not permanently ruin any of the relationships.

A feeling of familial identification as adoptees struggled with their feelings of belongingness, is described as a significant factor in the success of post-reunion experiences. Two birth mothers described their daughters as "moving in" and allying completely with the birth family. Other adoptees made it clear that they already had a family and insisted on distance from the biological clan. In most of the cases in this sample, adoptees are reported to maintain a presence in the adoptive family while becoming a presence in the birth family.

In evaluating their experiences, the birth mothers described in this book were between "happy" and "ecstatic" that they had a reunion with their offspring. However, the quality of the post-reunion experience was a combination of pleasure and pain. The authors conclude that there is no such thing as a perfect reunion because each emerges from the serious problems of a confidential adoption. They also conclude that there is no such thing as an easy post-reunion period because of the number of people involved and the intensity of the personality, history, conflicts, and uncertainties of each. At the same time, reunion and post-reunion experiences offer some birth mothers an opportunity for closure on their unfinished business with their children.

OUTCOME FOR BIRTH PARENTS

Over time, interested laypersons and professionals began to become concerned about the fate of birth parents after relinquishment of their child. Their stories began to emerge in self-reports and in organized research projects. The birth parent population is one in which confidentiality is often still important. The public case reports and research therefore carry heavy biases since they reflect the experiences primarily of those birth parents who feel strongly enough to give up their privacy and often join activist groups based on their strong feelings.

Even with this significant bias, the findings are illuminating since they so clearly challenge the myth that birth parents leave their problems behind them in the act of relinquishment. The birth parent literature consistently reports ongoing distress and reactions to the event as well as significant effects on new relationships.

Studies of a small number of birth mothers in psychiatric treatment note that the relinquishment of the child produced depressive phenomena and long-lasting preoccupation with the lost child.[16,17] While none of these women were referred for help because of the relinquishment per se, this life event proved to be a major factor in their subsequent experience.

Several larger surveys studied relinquishing parents who responded to newspaper requests for subjects or were members of a birth parent support group. In 1978 Sorosky, Baran, and Pannor[18] obtained interviews with 38 birth parents who responded to advertising. The relinquishments in this group generally occurred at an early age (14–18) the interval between the relinquishment and the study varied widely (1–33 years). Of these parents 50% reported continued feelings of grief and loss regarding their child; 82% expressed a desire for reunion.

In 1984 two large surveys of birth parents, mostly women, were conducted. Deykin and colleagues surveyed 334 members of Concerned United Birthparents (CUB), a national support group.[19] The researchers asked these parents to assess their psychological adjustment in regard to the marital relationships, fertility, and parenting. Respondents perceived the relinquishment as having a protracted negative influences on their lives in all these areas. They felt their marriages were stressed, particularly if they were married to the relinquished child's other parent. There was some, but not conclusive, evidence that they suffered from increased fertility problems. Moreover, most respondents reported that the relinquishing experience had a powerful effect on their parenting practices. They saw themselves as tending to be overprotective, compulsively worried about their children, and having difficulty accepting their children's growing independence. This study also investigated parents' desire to search for their child and found a significant correlation between the "primary reason" for the relinquishment and the decision to search. That is, parents who felt their relinquishment decision had been based on external pressure (such as finances) were significantly more likely to search than those who felt the decision was internal (wanting to finish school, unreadiness for parenting). Additionally, the greater the interval since the relinquishment, the greater the likelihood that a search would be initiated.

In a study reported in 1984 Winkler and van Keppel attempted to control some of the sampling biases present in previous studies by recruiting relinquishing mothers who were not members of a support group and by including a control group;[20] they also used standardized rating scales rather than questionnaires. The subjects were 213 women who had surrendered their children between the ages of 15 and 25, and the interval of time since relinquishment ranged from 4 to 20 years. The overall results of this study are consistent with others: effects of relinquishment are experienced as negative and long lasting. A "sense of loss" was reported by 50% of the participants. Psychological impairment was significantly more prevalent than in the matched sample. Factors considered major interferences to well-being were (1) absence of opportunities to talk through feelings about the relinquishment, (2) lack of social supports, and (3) an ongoing "sense of loss" about the child. This study suggests the need for counseling services for relinquishing mothers on an immediate and long-term basis.

The first major study of birth fathers was reported in 1988 and addressed some of the issues raised in the earlier Deykin survey.[21] A survey questionnaire was sent to 181 men who became known to the researchers through the media or through support groups. They had been between 12 and 43 years of age at the time of relinquishment, and 7 to 18 years had since elapsed. The survey studied search activity, marital interaction, and parenting functions. Overall, the results of this study support previous findings that surrender of a child remains a conflict-ridden issue. The majority of fathers maintained negative feelings about having participated in the adoption but, unlike birth mothers, few stated that having been a birth father had an impact on subsequent parenting. Responses to questions about effect on marital functioning were also less intense than those obtained in the Deykin survey of women. The researchers concluded that having been a birth father is not a predictor of the subsequent quality of marital functioning.

The most striking finding of the Deykin study of birth fathers had to do with motivation in searching behavior. While approximately the same proportion of birth mothers in the previous Deykin study and birth fathers in this study were searchers, their motivations were profoundly different. Birth mothers sought to comfort themselves with the assurance that the child was alive and well. Birth fathers embarked on a search with thoughts of retrieving the child. This pioneering study suggests that there may be significant gender differences in birth parent experiences. Hopefully, further research will shed more light on similarities and differences.

The methodological problems of these studies of birth parents are significant ones, but from them we have learned about those for whom the relinquishing experience has been so painful as to prompt them to seek support and acknowledgment of their anguish. We know very little about those who have not reached out in this way. We do not know how many of them are suffering in silence or how many feel they made a good decision, one that has not had a significant negative impact of their lives. From the latter we could learn more about the factors that contribute to coping skills and good psychological adjustment. In time, we will also learn more about how birth parents fare in adoption arrangements that include more openness.

CONCLUSION

The delineation of developmental tasks for birth parents and the available research findings—even with their significant biases and limitations—offer us information that can help birth parents toward successful mastery of their special tasks.

There are a number of real options in dealing with an unplanned pregnancy, any one of which can be successful. A woman can choose to abort. She can choose to keep and raise her child herself. She can keep parental rights but have some other adult take responsibility for raising the child. She can allow her child to be adopted by a family member or stranger.

It is of crucial importance that the birth mother take the opportunity to consider all possible options and make her decision on the basis of her *own* thoughts and feelings. We have become aware of the lifelong anguish felt by those who allowed themselves to make a decision based on others' judgments rather than their own. Pressures may come from the other biological parent, from the immediate or extended family, from friends, or from the social and legal systems. Any or all of these people may feel they know best. A birth mother must listen to others and inform herself of the possible ramifications of each choice, but her decision must be hers and hers alone in order for her to come to peace with it. Service providers need to support the birth mother in making a decision that feels right to her, even if her choice is not consistent with their judgment.

Any of the choices carries with it significant emotional burden. Each choice involves some degree or kind of regret. With an abortion decision, a mother regrets that she could not give her child life. A woman who chooses to keep and raise her child regrets that she is unable to offer better circumstances and regrets the compromises she must make in her own life in order to care for her child. A birth mother who makes an adoption plan regrets that she is not able to keep and raise her child.

These regrets are as real as the predominant feelings that tilt the balance toward the particular decision. It is necessary for birth parents to accept that this choice—like most others in life—has effects that will emerge variously over time. Such acceptance then allows them to recognize those effects as a natural and necessary part of the fabric of life.

General psychological literature describes healthy functioning as a balance between acknowledging, rather than repressing, one's conflicts and comforting oneself. For birth parents the acknowledgment and the comforting can take many forms. One form may be to allow oneself to mourn at significant times during the year and to otherwise devote one's energies to daily pursuits, which may include loving and raising other children. The birth mother takes comfort in knowing she took care of her relinquished child in the best way she could at the time. Another form might include regular correspondence or contact with the adoptive parents as a way of being assured of the child's well-being. Joining a group for birth parents may be valuable in sharing concerns and feelings; there may be great comfort in seeing that others struggle with similar issues.

When the necessary mourning does not diminish in frequency and intensity over time or when a birth parent continues to suffer repetitive anguish over the decision or exhibits consistent inexplicable behavior, this is an indication that a psychotherapeutic intervention is indicated (see chapter 6). Hopefully, through such an experience there can be a resumption of normal development.

The process of making one's own decision based on all possible options, accepting that any choice will inevitably produce short- and long-term effects that will become part of one's life, and then managing these effects in a balanced way contributes to transcendence into a new state of normalcy. Through this process a birth parent can best adapt to these challenging life circumstances.

CHAPTER 3

BECOMING PARENTS

*Developmental Tasks of Adoptive Mothers
and Fathers*

ADOPTION OCCURS in about 2–4% of all families in the United States. While there is no collection of data to give us actual statistics, it is generally observed that the majority of applicants for adoptive parenting are married infertile couples seeking an infant of similar background to their own. The diminishing availability of babies has necessitated pursuing the adoption of children who are foreign, older, or considered "hard to place" because of physical or emotional disabilities. A minority of applicants are fertile couples who wish for a child of a particular gender or wish to contribute to social welfare by providing a home for a needful child. The increasing number of available older and "hard to place" children, as well as the increasing pluralism in family structures, has contributed to greater flexibility in the requirements for those wishing to adopt these children; adoptive parents now include more single and gay people as well as those in need of financial subsidies to manage the raising of children.

Let us look at the experiences of those adoptive parents who form the majority: infertile couples who adopt infants of a similar background. Along the way we will note the similarities and differences in the experiences of those who adopt older or interracial children as well as examine the experiences of fertile parents.

Most people assume they will have a choice as to whether or not they will produce children. Many anticipate childbearing as an essential and significant part of their life experience. Girls while still very young begin talking about being mothers, looking at pregnant women, and imagining themselves pregnant one day. They stuff pillows under their sweatshirts to see how they might look; pajama parties, dormitory rooms, and ladies' lunches are all common settings for sharing fantasies of what it will feel like—some day. Many men look forward to the pride of siring progeny. They imagine themselves as proud fathers walking beside their resplendently pregnant mates and later pushing a baby carriage filled with prime stock.

When a couple finds themselves unable to bear a child, it is often a watershed for them as individuals and as a couple. A basic confidence in being able to control important aspects of one's life is shattered. "How could this happen?" "Why us?" "We want children so much while others don't want them at all!" "This is so unfair. Are we being punished for something?" "We did everything we were supposed to—what's the use of trying hard anymore?" When it becomes clear that their first choice—to bear their own biological children—is not available to them, the couple must change their attitude set about the structure of their family. What was once thought to be a clear-cut yes (we want children) or no (we don't want children) question now becomes more complex. New options must be considered. The couple can choose to remain childless or can choose to pursue a variety of methods to achieve parenthood. Today these methods include in vitro procedures using a donor egg, where the woman carries an embryo conceived outside of the womb and then implanted in her own womb to develop naturally; artificial insemination, where sperm is acquired from a donor, thereby producing a partially biological child; or surrogate mothering, where another woman agrees to carry the partial or fully biological child of the couple. Or the couple can adopt a child outside either of their own bloodlines. For most couples these options do not fulfill their original expectations or constitute their first choice.

When the choice is made to adopt a child, the couple faces the internal and external ramifications of this decision. They struggle within themselves, with each other, and with family and society at large as they attempt to achieve the experience of parenthood that has been denied them biologically.

In his pioneering work of the 1950s David Kirk studied social attitudes toward adoptive parents and found that the biological foundation for parenthood was widely considered a necessary condition for "parental role performance."[1] He also found that being an adoptive parent was neither clearly defined nor fully sanctioned. He concluded that adoptive parents were not afforded the same kinds of cultural goods and supports as were biological parents. The celebration of a pregnancy, baby showers, and the experience of being catered to were not part of an adoptive parent's preparation. Even the adoptive parent's complaints about the stresses and strains of ongoing parenting could be heard differently since it involved someone else's biological child.

Adoptive parents thus suffer from the trauma of being deprived of bearing their own children and from the handicap of a social norm that presumes bloodline to be an inviolate and preferable tie. Kirk was the first to emphasize the need to appreciate the differences between the biological and the adoptive parenting experience rather than deny them. He suggested that such denial increases the possibility of emotional interferences with parent-child, marital, family, and social relationships. Conversely, he saw recognition of and attention to these differences as contributory to better personal and social adjustment.

Since the 1950s we have begun to understand more about the ways in which adoptive parenting is at once similar to and profoundly different from the nonadoptive experience. Professionals have come to recognize the need, consistent with Kirk's ideas, for adoptive parents to actively attend to and master the additional tasks of adoptive parenting. In so doing, they can experience not only the mixture of pleasure and pain common to all parents but the satisfaction of mastering those aspects of parenting that are unique in the adoptive family.

Under ordinary circumstances couples go through a series of life stages related to childbearing. Sometimes an unplanned pregnancy precedes the decision to bear a child; this pregnancy can be entirely accidental or an "accident on purpose" as a couple drifts into parenting. Often there is first a decision to bear a child, which is followed by an attempt to become pregnant, achievement of a pregnancy, gestation, and child birth. Finally, couples experience stages of the child's development from infancy through adulthood.

With adoptive parents, a sharp variation in the pattern occurs. They never drift into parenthood. The attempts to become pregnant are *not* followed by successful childbirth. Instead, what follows is the traumatic recognition of infertility, a clear, active decision to pursue adoption, the adoption process, the adoption itself, and then the experience of parenting throughout the child's developmental stages. Not only is there a variant interlude in becoming parents but this variant affects the content and process of all subsequent stages despite the fact that these stages are, in name, the same as they are for nonadoptive parents. What are the additional tasks required of adoptive parents and what do they need to do to master them successfully?

PHASE 1: THE COUPLE'S DECISION TO ADOPT

The decision to adopt a child requires sufficient acceptance of one's inability to reproduce to make adoption feel like a necessary, viable, and acceptable alternative. This process of acceptance is most often a very painful and lonely one. It is equivalent to the process of accepting other physical handicaps, but it is different in that it tends not to elicit the same kind of empathy and validation as do other disabilities.[2] In an effort to be supportive, friends and family may be quick to come up with immediate solutions that show little understanding of the hard and brutal fact that the problem of infertility can never be "solved," will never go away, and will remain in the hearts and minds of the couple forever. We will later see the ways in which feelings about infertility affect the process of adopting as well as the subsequent relationship with the child.

In her article "There's Always Adoption," Diane Renne describes the process of grieving of nonproductive couples.[3] She notes the lack of validation couples often feel in their grieving period. They tend to think they have no right to feel so bad: they don't have cancer; they haven't lost the ability to see, hear, walk, or talk. Because their suffering feels unique and somehow unjustified, it can become quite secret and go underground.

Renne describes four stages of grieving: *shock, protest, despair,* and *resolution.* She describes couples in the state of shock as mustering their defenses in an attempt to deny the emerging painful reality. They rationalize and avoid and continue to look for a way out: they decide the problem is that they have been working too hard, that they need a vacation so they can have successfully productive sex. Infertility cannot be happening to them; it is temporary and will surely work itself out in time.

But the problem does not go away. The couple move into a period of protest, refusing to accept the continuing confirmation of their infertility. No matter what doctors say, they will find a way. They try harder and concentrate all their energy on attempting to establish the optimal circumstances. They may become quite single-minded in focusing on the monthly cycle, with other parts of their lives fading in contrast. Each failure makes it more difficult to deny the problem and muster a new act of protestation. With time, they cannot help but fall into a state of despair. Realistic hope is now abandoned. Instead, there is pain, depression, and helplessness. They recognize that they have failed to fulfill what they had felt was an essential function of their lives. Feelings of inadequacy, guilt, and blame emerge. It is a natural human defense to try to replace guilt with blame in attempting to not feel so responsible. Blame is sometimes directed at one's partner ("If we had started earlier like *I* wanted to"), at doctors ("They could have done more"), or at the world in general ("Everything bad happens to me"). Confidence in one's sense of masculinity or femininity is threatened, normal activity is interrupted, it is difficult to go on with everyday life. The individual differences in the course of this process will soon tax the marital relationship, leaving each partner even more alone in the struggle.

Once the couple has succumbed to the despair of their grief, they can begin to emerge from it. When they have shed enough tears, felt enough rage, practiced emotionally beating themselves and each other sufficiently, each partner can begin to reorganize and approach acceptance and resolution. Then the couple can begin to do so as well. They can renew their positive sense of themselves despite the reproductive problems, recognize what they have to offer each other and a child, and ready themselves for the tasks that have unexpectedly become necessary if they are to enlarge their family through adoption.

Expanding on Renne's work, we can see that the road to this acceptance, in length and intensity, may vary from couple to couple, may be different for men and women, and may involve still other issues for the unreproductive partner, if one is so identified. Historically, all societies have valued both men's and women's reproductive abilities and perceived children as wealth. Women deemed barren were sometimes banished. Beyond the social deficit is the intensity of each person's own need to reproduce. One factor is the degree to which one's identity is related to being a parent and what individual needs one might have to be a biological parent per se.

Katherine, a woman who had been a very lonely only child,

daydreamed from childhood about one day marrying and having six children. In contrast to what she felt was her parents' "stingy" production of one child, she planned an effusive production of children, each more beautiful than the last, all reflecting some part of herself. She would hold them and love them. She would never be lonely again, nor would they since they would always have each other. The news of her own infertility struck as "a knife in [her] heart." She could not even measure up to her parents' stingy production. She thought she would feel lonely forever. Her infertility tapped into so many poignant issues for her that it was years before she was able to recover and reorganize sufficiently to even begin thinking about other options.

By contrast, here is Marie, a woman whose parents divorced when she was a toddler. Her mother remarried a year later to a man who became a devoted father with whom Marie enjoyed a warm and close relationship throughout her childhood and into adulthood. After suffering several miscarriages, Marie finally required a hysterectomy. Throughout her experience of disappointment and grieving, she retained a sense of comfort in the possibility of adopting. Her real experience of a wonderfully satisfying relationship with a nonbiological father let her know that a fulfilling adoption experience was possible. For her, becoming a biological parent was not crucial.

When reproductive difficulties have been identified in only one of the partners, acceptance is still necessary in both. At least some period of stress in the relationship is to be expected. A large component of this stress is related to the many aspects of this problem that may seem unspeakable. For everyday marital problems the couple can "duke it out" with whatever differences of opinion there may be. It can be an up-front, on-the-line fight. How forthright they can be depends on the sensitivity of the issues for them individually and as a couple. Some manage conflicts about money, in-laws, housework, and recreation just fine while others rate any one of these as an explosive issue. Few couples find sexual problems an easy topic to discuss, and reproduction is closely related. Reproductive issues touch on sensitive matters of a personal nature; with such potential for hurtfulness it is a wonder so many infertile couples survive so well. How, for example, is the fertile partner to struggle with the understandable disappointment in the spouse and the inevitable question of whether he or she wants a biological child more than the marriage? This partner must confront thoughts and feelings that feel personally unacceptable, even unspeakable to the mate or to others:

"How would I feel if I knew she was thinking of leaving *me* because I was infertile? What a horrible thing to be thinking."
"I must not be a very good person at heart."
"Does this mean I don't really love him?"
"Did I marry her to have children and now that she's failed, am I dumping her?"
"I don't want anyone to ever know I've had such thoughts."
"He tells me to say how I feel; I could never say this to him."
"I wonder if she really knows?"

These are all common but usually secret thoughts.

Both partners, but especially the nonreproductive one, struggle with disappointment. It is simply very difficult to accept the physical fact of infertility and still maintain a high level of self-esteem. In the depths of despair Tony, a 35-year-old man, confided:

> I can't believe this is true of me. What kind of a man am I? She says she doesn't think of me any differently, but I wonder if it's true. She seems distant and cool; sex certainly is not as much fun. I wonder if she's thinking of leaving me? Would I think of leaving her under the same circumstances? I have certainly let her down—she has every right to want to leave. I'm not much to stay for. Is this more important than all the other good parts of our relationship? We certainly have lost touch with all that we both are besides reproductive. I hope some day despite this, we can regain all we once had with each other.

The quality of the couple's sexual relationship varies through all these stages. The stage of attempting a pregnancy can become highly stressed and mechanical, with each partner trying to do the right thing at the right time. When the impossibility or improbability of pregnancy is recognized, sex may feel like a reminder of the failure and may be avoided. The ability to enjoy sexuality for its own sake can come only with emotional healing.

There may also be gender differences in the significance of childbearing to the individual, which may make it difficult for men and women to understand each other's feelings and reactions. A recent study of 275 infertile couples found that women bear most of the stress associated with infertility, even when it is their husbands who are infertile.[4] The researchers noted that the focus on the woman's body as the couple attempts conception, including the depressing evidence of reproductive failure indicated by menstruation, exacerbated this stress.

While a man is deprived of the satisfaction of contributing to a pregnancy and bearing a biological child, his mate is deprived of the experience of pregnancy itself. They thus have different losses to mourn. The wish for the experience of pregnancy and childbirth is stronger in some women than in others. For some, these experiences may be seen as a strong bond to an abstracted "female experience" and hence as a necessary link to other women, especially those within their family. These women may feel a real pang of agony each time they hear of another woman's pregnancy or childbirth. They may never be able to attend a baby shower with genuine pleasure or welcome another woman's baby without some degree of anxious pain. As with other forms of mourning, the feeling of loss may never be completely over, though the intensity and frequency of the pain diminishes over time. Other women may not feel such deprivation and loss and will be less involved in this kind of continued mourning process. It may be difficult for many men to understand and accept these needs and wishes; for some it will be particularly difficult if there is also a sense of responsibility for depriving their mate of an experience that is clearly very important to her.

John M. was at first devastated at the diagnosis of his sterility. As time passed and the couple explored opportunities for adoption, he became reassured that they would someday have children. He became happily optimistic whereas his wife, Jane, remained sad and embittered. John found himself unsympathetic and resentful toward her. He could not understand why she was still so unhappy since they would have children, which is what she said she wanted. Given his responsibility for their infertility, it was hard for John to acknowledge his wife's disappointment. At her request, he was able to give her more time to grieve. He even came to understand the ways in which this loss was more profound for her than for him. Without this kind of communication the couple might easily have become mired in resentment and estrangement.

The pain of dealing with reproductive problems evokes several underlying issues that often become confused. Distinguishing them and keeping them separate is essential to a genuine readiness to adopt a child. Nonreproductive individuals and couples often, at least temporarily, confuse reproduction, sexual adequacy, and the competency to parent. This confusion reflects social attitudes as well, since the phrase *barren woman* still carries with it the image of an ungiving, empty, unmaternal person and words such as *infertility*, meaning the inability to reproduce, and *impotency*, meaning the inability to achieve erection and ejaculation, are frequently mistakenly interchanged. Despite the extensive dissemination of information regarding causes of infertility and its irrelevance to sexuality, popular culture still reflects a merged view of these functions and the diminution if not stigmatization of those involved. Men's locker-room banter still includes expressions like "shooting blanks" or otherwise not "making it." While times have changed from the days when women were held solely responsible for reproduction, popular social attitudes tend to compound the couple's confusion and their feelings of loss of status. An infertile man may, for a time, feel that he is less potent, less manly, and thus less capable of being a father. A woman may feel that because she is unable to become pregnant, she is somehow less feminine and/or less able to become a "real" mother. She feels left out of the mothers' group among her friends.

As the couple experiences disappointment in themselves or in each other, they may begin to confuse the issues at the core of their disappointment. In processing reproductive problems, they may feel a loss of the mate as a complete man or complete woman. This can be a self-fulfilling prophesy. Sexual excitement, for example, may be compromised by anger and disappointment over reproductive problems. There may have been so much clinical attention to the reproductive organs and so much tension around sexual acts that either or both partners at times feel a need for a respite from thinking or doing anything about their sexual relationship. At other times they may need the physical comfort of sexual intimacy or reassurance from each other but may still avoid sexual relations. These needs may also emerge at different times and therefore may result in one partner's initiative being turned down by the other—at a time when flagging self-esteem can least afford it. In these instances a partner might conclude that he or she is no longer an attractive or good lover. Tension over the reproductive problem may produce a kind of general irritability and impatience. In such a state of disequilibrium, either or both partners may be vulnerable to seeking comfort, distraction, or relief through other sexual partners, alcohol or other drugs, overworking, or too much recreation. This kind of acting out usually contributes to further distress rather than resolution.

Going outside the home for comfort and support does not always help. Visiting friends or family members with children may stir up more tension and irritability. Despite (and because of) their longings for a child, either or both partners may find themselves so uncomfortable with a child's presence that they may feel irritated with the child. They may end up "proving" to themselves and to their partner that they would not be good parents anyway. Many years and three adopted children after experiencing feelings like these, Sally admits: "When I look back at those terrible times, I shudder to see how confused we were and how, in that confusion, we hurt ourselves and hurt each other so blindly. I don't know what could have made it any different—whether anyone else could have helped us with it. It now seems like something we had to experience ourselves and find our way through."

Yet the important thing to realize is that it is natural for couples to go through this process of confusion. Sorting out the differences between reproduction, sexual adequacy, and competency to parent is difficult and disorienting. Hopefully, however, with attention to these issues and with the healing that time allows, it will eventually become clear that lack of reproductive ability has no inherent relation to sexual adequacy or to the ability to parent competently.

Denise L. was an attractive professional woman who took pride in her strong body. When it became clear that there was no effective treatment for her infertility, her relationship to her body shifted. It now felt empty and useless. She was convinced that her husband was no longer attracted to her, and she withdrew sexually. Feeling so inadequate physically also made her doubt her competency in other areas. She was not sure she could do anything very well anymore—including being a mother. Mr. L. tried to offer loving support but often despaired of his wife's unhappiness with herself. Gradually, with support from family and friends, Denise was able to reinstate a realistic view of herself: her womb was empty but her body was whole; she was the same person she had been prior to the diagnosis of infertility. She was ready to again enjoy being a lover and was ready to open her heart to a child.

Like those with any developmental vulnerability, either partner of an infertile couple may fall prey to confusion at times of stress, and the differentiation between reproduction, sexuality, and parenting will need to be clarified again for a continued sense of well-being and good functioning. As they experience clarity out of their confusion and accept the reproductive problems for what they are—no more and no less—the partners prepare themselves for parenting and adopting a child.

The decision to adopt children outside the family's bloodline may trigger thoughts and feelings in the couple that they did not even know it was possible for them to have. Issues of class, ethnicity, and religion may emerge as new and more powerful forces than were previously apparent as the couple confronts the reality of a lack of genealogical continuity. There is a recognition that the biological chain that links one generation to the next, from the past to the future, will have a missing link.

The continuous link will be the psychological relationship that will carry on the family history. This psychological relationship will reflect the kinds of bonds, values, interests, and traditions that this new family develops. What are the limits, if any, of the kind of child who can become a viable link in this psychological family? Can he be of another race or religious background? Can she look significantly different from the family? When the moment of truth arrives, the partners may each find themselves surprised at their own responses. They may feel more inclusive than they would ever have imagined. "I was amazed at how little the baby's background or biological parents mattered," said one woman. "I've always been a kind of fussy person, but in this case I didn't feel fussy at all." More likely, they may discover some deep-seated biases that may be difficult to acknowledge. "I can't believe this of myself," said Michael, a man who had always credited himself with being of liberal mind, "but I'm finding myself very uncomfortable with the idea of a child from a black family. It seems so unfair to reject an innocent baby because of his color, but I have to admit it makes me uncomfortable. I'm afraid I couldn't feel as much like his real father as I would like to." In a similarly apologetic way, an applicant for adoption "confessed" that she really wanted a baby born of a mother of her own religion. She said this seemed strange to her since she was not a religiously observant person, but she had to admit that only such a child would feel "familiar" to her. Couples are sometimes reluctant to share these feelings with adoption agencies for fear of having themselves viewed negatively and thus reducing their chances of obtaining a child—not such an easy task these days.

Experiencing unacceptable feelings can contribute to an increased sense of guilt for having feelings, which naturally and understandably evolve from one's own experiences.

There may also be surprises as members of the extended family respond to the issue of adoption. In some families there is a great deal of pressure exerted by the elders to have offspring in order to increase family size and to carry on the family name. Small families that may have been decimated by war or illness may have few potential reproductive agents to save them from extinction. Men and women who find themselves incapable of fulfilling the need for the family may equate biological parenthood with the parenting experience itself. They may never be able to afford themselves the pleasure of psychological parenting, the permanent emotional attachment to and the care of children, through adoption.

A couple from a close, strict Irish Catholic family dreaded informing the family of a planned adoption of a child not of the same origins. They were delightfully surprised with the family's warm and supportive acceptance of the plan. "A baby is a baby," they said, "and can be raised just as good an Irish Catholic as anyone else." They welcomed the child wholeheartedly. This unconditional acceptance may be more difficult for families with rigid religious or racial definitions. Another couple had no concerns about their very liberal family's ability to accept a non-blood child and were distressed to find themselves confronted with suspicious questions about the child's background, a suspiciousness that persisted throughout the child's upbringing. As the couple and their extended families confront the fact of genealogical discontinuity, they learn more about themselves, their needs, and their wishes. Through this awareness, they begin to prepare a place for the new family member. This place must be one that recognizes the child as a family member of equal status, with full rights and privileges.

Extended families will vary in their ability to immediately embrace a non-blood child depending on how important genealogical continuity is to them and how well they are able to adapt to these new circumstances. Their resistance is likely to make it more difficult for the couple to make the necessary shifts to prepare themselves for initiating the adoption process.

Studies of gender requests in adoption find a significant preference for girls over boys. Some observers have interpreted this as a reluctance to pass the family name down by means of a nonbiological child. Others have interpreted it as the dominance of the adopting mother's preference for daughters, particularly where there is a chance this may be the only child. At this point, all parties are dealing with an abstract notion of an "adopted child." It is not possible to foresee the child as a real person who makes his or her own relationships in the immediate and extended family, and often melts away even some of the harshest resistances.

PHASE 2: THE ADOPTION PROCESS

Initiating an adoption process—in any form—publicly reveals the couple's failure at reproduction. This exposure and the responses it elicits may open barely healed wounds or at least cause twinges of pain over the ongoing issues. People can intentionally and unintentionally say and do hurtful things in connection with adoption. A couple may hear horror tales of unsuccessful adoptions by cautioning friends. They may experience overly sympathetic family members who treat the inability to bear children as an irrecoverable tragedy and failure. They may have to field inappropriately personal and insensitive questions such as "What's wrong?" or "Whos fault is it?" At the same time, they are likely to experience much genuine support and enthusiasm for the decision to adopt.

Once the decision to adopt a child is made, the couple scans their community for resources. Currently, they will find that most established agencies maintain long waiting lists for infants and also have firm requirements regarding age limits, health, and finances. For some people, the length of the waiting list places them at risk for not meeting the age requirement when a baby would become available to them. Couples then struggle with the question of whether to consider adopting a child who is more readily available through an agency, for example, an older, interracial, or handicapped child. Some couples decide to pursue private adoptions either because they do not meet agency requirements or because they seek adoption practices and resources that differ from those available to them through agencies. There are six states (Connecticut, Delaware, Michigan, Minnesota, Maryland, and North Dakota) that prohibit private adoptions. Residents of these states need to find ways of using facilitators in other states in order to arrange a private adoption. Even in those states where private adoptions are legal, the small number of children available may require potential adopters to explore resources in other countries. Making such arrangements requires a great deal of time and energy as well as substantial financial means.

In some areas interested potential parents have banded together to help each other with the demanding and often demoralizing adoption process. For example, several couples in Detroit created The Family Tree, a group to help couples navigate resources and bureaucratic mazes.

As the couple pursues their goal, they are required to open themselves up to public scrutiny as no biological parent is required to do. In an agency adoption they will find themselves in an intensely competitive situation. It is not sufficient to be deemed a "good enough" couple; they must be the best of the lot, judged to be least likely to fail as parents. Characteristics over which they have no control such as age, health, and financial resources are subject to scrutiny. Personal qualities of stability and the nature of the marital relationship and the couple's relationships with the extended family are the kind of factors whose assessment is left up to the subjective judgments of agency evaluators. Applicants will no doubt feel confused about the criteria used to judge them and highly anxious about how their profile measures up.

One real problem in this phase of the adoption process is that the partners individually and together have been, and still are, in the midst of a serious life crisis. How they appear at this moment and how they have been in recent times is not an accurate portrayal of their "pre–baby problem" state of existence. Questioned about the quality of their marital relationship, the couple may have difficulty answering with any degree of honesty. They may fear revealing the depths of despair they have felt about each other. They may find it difficult to explain the disturbances in sexual pleasure in a way that would not be interpreted as problematic. A couple may well entertain the following unspoken thoughts during an interview:

> How can we sit here and say our marriage is strong, we have a good sex life, and we will make good parents? Only six months ago we were at each other's throats, thinking of splitting up. We know we have come a long way in a short time, but *they* may not think so. Maybe there are couples that held hands and defied adversity together, surrounded by an understanding, loving family. If so, they certainly will be chosen over us.

Comparing themselves to an idealized, unreal, too-good-to-be-true couple, they may be fearful about the evaluator's reactions and consciously or unconsciously edit important information about themselves.

Moreover, it is increasingly common for birth parents to have significant influence (if not the final decision) on the selection of parents for their child. Again, potential adoptive parents are open to scrutiny and may be rejected competitively (for not having as much education or financial security as another couple, for example) or even idiosyncratically. One couple harbored a birth mother in their home beginning in the sixth month of her pregnancy. The agreement was that the couple would support her, including medical care and counseling, through the birth and relinquishment of her baby to them. They had already successfully adopted a child in this manner three years before. All seemed well until the beginning of the ninth month, when the birth mother decided she did not want to relinquish the child to *them.* Despite the fact that she liked them and thought they were good people and that their older child appeared to be thriving, she found their home too different from the one she had grown up in and ultimately placed her baby with a family more similar to her own. The couple was devastated by her rejection.

This process of evaluation and public review can stir up anxiety about personal competency to be a parent, along with concerns that may still exist about the partner. Each partner may hold the other responsible in some way for the failure to be selected. In fact, it may well be true that some characteristic of one of them is responsible for the rejection. A woman who works full-time outside the home may be judged less desirable than a full-time homemaker, for example. The problems come when responsibility is turned into blame. As with other relevant issues, the partners need to confront themselves and each other, sorting out the external realities and moving from blame to mutual support in this highly stressful process. When a couple finally receives validation of their competency to become parents, they can enjoy the affirmation of their potential parenting, which then confirms their self-regard. This confirmation is a bonus that adoptive parents have over nonadoptive parents: as stressful as the public scrutiny may be, getting an ''A'' in potential parenting from a rigorous board of examiners or from the birth mother herself can be taken to heart and recognized as a genuine vote of confidence.

At the same time that this preparation and affirmation are occurring, the mourning process itself continues. As the couple conceptualizes the creation of the child to be adopted, they must increasingly come to terms with the loss of bloodline and loss of their fantasized biological child. Most people imagine that they will bear a child with their best (and perhaps even improved-upon) features, but there is also the concern that the child will have their worst. All of these feelings are very personal since they reflect prospective parents' natural narcissistic needs. No real child meets any parent's idealized fantasies, and all parents experience some disappointment in their children. But the wishes are as real as the disappointments that often follow them. The idea that one's child is not likely to bear any physical resemblance to oneself and, in fact, has no biological inheritance is a jolting realization. ''As far back as I can remember,'' Martha reported,

> I had an image of the little girl I would have some day. She would be tall and strong (like me) with thick, dark hair (unlike my mousy brown color). She'd win the prizes I never won; I'd be by her side to urge her on. Now I see it is likely to be very different. My adopted child could have blond hair or dark skin or even be short and plump. I know that I can love any child we bring home, but it is hard saying good-bye to that other little girl; she's been with me so long it makes me sad to think about her.

Adoptive parents will each have their own version of their idealized child and will need to mourn its loss many times in many ways over the course of a lifetime. There is no inherent difficulty in the fact that there is an image of a fantasized biological child or that it is necessary for the loss of this child to be mourned. Nonadoptive parents go through a similar problem when their own biological children do not measure up to their wishes. The difficulty arises when an idealized child is not recognized and mourned and is unconsciously imposed on the real child—adopted *or* biological—who can never be seen and appreciated fully for who he or she is. Under these circumstances parents live in a state of constant disappointment, and children, sensing this disappointment, feel they are not the person they are supposed to be, thus fostering feelings of inferiority and illegitimacy.

Even after being chosen for adoptive parenting, actually attaining possession of a child can be troublesome. With more openness and more options available to birth parents, we are more frequently observing the phenomenon of incompleted placements. At the extreme, adoptive parents may meet with birth parents during the pregnancy, attend the birth, hold the baby, and then find that the parents have decided not to relinquish the child. Some couples have gone through more than one such experience before they achieve a completed adoption. These couples must struggle with profound disappointment. They must also grieve the loss of the child they had imagined would be theirs, a child they perhaps even met and held. Some couples have likened this experience to a stillbirth; surely it has all the related emotions. A couple will need time to recover from this loss before they feel ready to welcome another child into their lives.

PHASE 3: THE ADOPTIVE FAMILY IS BORN

When at last the child is theirs, the couple finally enjoys the fruits of their labors. The empty crib or bed is occupied, the house is aflutter with any number of adults trying to attend to the needs of one child, the arms of parents who waited so long are now filled. There may be an atmosphere of great relief and accomplishment, with friends and family sharing this sense of triumph over adversity. There is a child where there was none. The problem is solved.

Or is it? Perhaps underneath the excitement and the adoptive parents' feelings of success in finally achieving the adoption is the knowledge that somewhere there are grieving birth parents who will forever be a kind of presence in their household. Even if there has not been any personal contact and the biological parents remain phantoms, there may be a sense that there are people out there thinking, wondering, hoping, and missing their child despite their commitment to relinquishment.

While there is a variation in the intensity of this awareness, adoptive parents cannot forget these people, nor can they ignore the kind of promise they made to them in the act of assuming responsibility for the child. There may be many times when they think, "If only they knew how wonderful she is they would never have given her away" or "We have not been able to be very good parents" or "If they knew how this would turn out, they would have kept him." A child's birthday or legal adoption day is a time when these thoughts and feelings may be even more intense. Mary R. spoke about the difficult times around her children's birthdays:

I begin getting depressed and anxious feelings as soon as I start planning their birthday celebrations. I feel sad for their birth mothers because I know what they are missing. I am sure they think about the children on these special days. At the same time, I feel anxious about producing a perfect day. It may seem odd, but on that day I feel the birth mother is seeing everything that happens. I want her to see a happy, healthy child. I hope with time I will relax more and be able to enjoy the day with its normal ups and downs.

Whatever the circumstances, adoptive parents and birth parents remain a presence in each other's lives as their mutual child grows.

Even though the hope and anticipation of adoption may have continued over many years, there are also some ways in which adoptive parents are thrust into an "instant parenthood" that is different from the experience of biological parents. For one thing, they do not have the experience of the increasing physical presence of the fetus for nine months. Nor do they have the social confirmation as people note the progress of the pregnancy and inquire about the baby's well-being. Too often, there is no baby shower, and parenting classes have only recently been offered for adopting couples. These are important markers of the birth process, each of which contributes to preparing for the child's arrival.

The child arrives complete with his or her own genetic base and unique prenatal, birth, and separation experiences. He or she comes to a couple who have done their best to resolve their own grief and to ready their home to welcome him or her. As in a biological family, there is at once the issue of a temperament match. Well-known researchers have studied the temperament and development of children on a long-term basis and have concluded that the "goodness of fit" between parents and child is a more significant factor in adjustment than the temperament of the child himself.[5] This goodness of fit is often unpredictable: a quiet couple may find a lively, energetic child refreshing and stimulating, or they may find him irritating and overwhelming. No one knows if the odds for goodness of fit are significantly different between adoptive and nonadoptive families.

One recent study of the attachment of adoptive children who had been placed as infants found no differences in attachment between adoptive and nonadoptive mother–infant dyads.[6] The authors concluded that "lack of early contact per se does not place middle-class adoptive families at risk for the development of anxious mother–infant relationships." As might be expected, the insecurely attached adopted infants had experienced significantly more foster placements before adoption than the securely attached adopted infants. Some studies suggest that the impact of early aversive experiences can fade away when children have the opportunity to form new positive attachments and that children are not necessarily scarred for life by early traumas and deprivation.[7,8,9] So we see that an early attachment situation involves a constellation of factors whose combinations range from ready, unconflicted adoptive parents, an untraumatized child, and a good temperament match all the way to anxious, conflicted parents, a traumatized child, and a poor temperament match. There is thus a wide possible range of early attachment experiences.

With the placement of the child there is excitement that is often tempered with apprehension. Since so much energy has been invested in achieving this homecoming, can it possibly live up to the intensity of its anticipation? The single-minded goal of the adoption may inhibit expression of some normal ambivalence and disappointment. When parents feel that they have spent so much emotionally, physically, and financially to bring home a child, it may be hard to admit any mixed feelings to themselves or others. Thoughts like "I sure hate to give up my peaceful nights" may remain secret. There may be more of a tendency, at least publicly, to idealize and see the adoption only as a dream come true. The couple and others may, accurately or not, view the child as looking just like a parent or other family member. Some realities may make this effort at normalization difficult. Many people bring home a baby who may have traveled far and may be exhausted, disoriented, and even sick. This does not fit the perfect picture very well. As with all parents, there will also be some conscious or unconscious matching of the real child to the fantasized child. While biological parents may feel freer to express their disappointments ("I really wish it had been a girl"; "I was hoping for a calmer, quieter baby"; "I can't believe he does not have my red hair"), adoptive parents may feel they should be grateful for what they got and may not be able to express normal disappointment.

There are also times, however, when an adopted child meets a need or a wish that a biological child did not or would have been unlikely to meet. A child adopted by fertile parents seeking a particular gender is one example. And some adopted children may be perceived as more attractive, brighter, more talented, or better tempered than the parents imagine themselves, or their fantasized offspring, to be. One adoptive mother had always felt her blue eyes were her best (and perhaps only good) feature. She lamented the fact that her husband had dark brown eyes, which were likely to dominate in their offspring. The arrival of an adopted baby boy with gleaming deep blue eyes seemed like an impossible wish come true and contributed to a feeling that this child was, in fact, better than any child the couple themselves could have produced. This match (or mismatch) may help or hinder the beginnings of the bonding process and contribute significantly to basic attitudes in the attachment. However, over-valuing and aggrandizing a child for features that may be related to the fantasized child does the child no more justice than under-valuing or penalizing him or her for other features. Parent and child need to come to know each other realistically rather than in comparison to images or fantasies.

It is not uncommon for adoptive parents to experience some period of post-homecoming blues. This may be related to the expenditure of energy needed in arranging for the adoption, emotional fatigue, continued mourning for their first choice—the perfect biological child—or a combination of any number of issues common to the adoption process. The attitudes of extended family and friends may ameliorate or exacerbate these blues with their helpful or not so helpful comments and behavior. "I am giving your baby a savings bond, just like all the others" said one aunt. This kind of comment delivers a covert message that this child is different and connotes a lesser status in her mind for the adopted child that can be hard to confront. On the face of it, the aunt is doing the right thing. It is certainly better than refusing to give the gift because the child is not a blood relative. But the message is a clear and not so subtle reminder that the formation of this family is not what it is supposed to be.

These reminders are quick to revive the couple's painful wishes for their first choice. Some family members and friends may say how lucky the new mother is not to have had to suffer through a labor and delivery, or they may perpetuate the myth that adopting a child increases their chances of pregnancy.[10] Others may be genuinely loving and supportive and able to accept the differences along with the couple and focus now on attaching to and including this new family member.

As routines of daily life develop, the couple begins experiencing parenthood. However warm or cool the beginnings may be, however easy or difficult the bonding process, the couple find themselves completely responsible for the welfare of the new child and for fulfilling all the necessary roles and functions. They busily supply the household with necessities. They feel the child's body against their own. They become familiar with the child's sounds and smells. They learn what works and what does not work as they care for him. They take pleasure in a successful feeding, a good bowel movement, or a fleeting smile. They worry about colic, a sniffle, or spitting up. As the child thrives, so do they. They take pride in the child who is thriving because of their parenting. They may even begin to feel that characteristics often thought to be genetic—like the child's good looks, pleasant disposition, and alert mind—are the result of their good care.

They begin to feel like parents and emotionally claim their child. Adoptive mothers begin sharing their anxieties about child care with their mothers, sisters, and friends, and new bonds based on their roles as mothers may begin to occur. Grandparents begin doting, and siblings of the parents may begin to enjoy being aunts and uncles. While all the difficult issues continue to exist and will still need to be dealt with, the daily life of parenting, with all its joys and woes, is a very real experience of adoptive parents.

Through this daily experience, adoptive parents begin the process of recognizing and accepting the significance of psychological bonding and social expressions of parenthood. Members of the extended family, in turn, realign themselves around the new family member, forming their own particular relationship with the child and the growing nuclear family unit. One grandfather commented, ''I have to admit that becoming a grandfather for the first time was hard for me and especially hard because the child was to be adopted. I wasn't sure I wanted any part of it. I'm afraid I didn't make it any easier for the kids and what they were going through. But that little girl just warmed her way into my heart. I had never felt like such a sucker for anyone in my life. I love being a grandfather.'' Just as in all families, some extended family members will be closer to the child than will others, and some distance may be maintained by those still resistant to the novel, non-blood, relationship.

As adoptive parents live more and more in the world of parenthood, they may be periodically jolted by others' attitudes that may reflect a perception and judgment that the couple does not share with comments such as ''It is so good of you to take in a homeless child.'' Again, they may be confronted with inappropriate questions such as ''What do you know about her parents?'' There can be similar discomfort when a conversation turns to the topic of pregnancy and delivery and the adoptive parents feel marginalized. ''I feel a little ridiculous sitting there wishing I had stretch marks to exhibit,'' said one woman. ''At the same time, I wonder if they can really understand that when my baby rests on my shoulder in the middle of the night, he could not feel more like my own flesh and blood.'' Like this woman, all adoptive parents need to find their own way of enjoying the reality of parenting while regretting the circumstances that make it in some ways different and often more difficult.

Adoptive parents who have their own biological children experience some of the same challenges confronting nonfertile adoptive couples as well as those unique to their special situation. When they choose to adopt a child who may not be an infant and may have experienced other placements they too are plunged into a stage of instant parenthood for which they have had little preparation. As these parents become involved in the child's daily life, they begin their own real parenting experience and attachment to this particular child. Moreover, they too deal with extended family and community attitudes toward adoption. They may find themselves under scrutiny for favoring either the biological or the adopted child and may constantly be trying to compensate, sometimes by overcompensating. They may sometimes feel they have sacrificed the well-being of their biological child in attempting to meet the special needs of the adoptee. Interracial adoptions can complicate the picture further since the adopted child is so clearly distinguished. While their intention is to provide well for a child in need, they sometimes suffer from social critics who have concerns about removing children from their ethnic and cultural origins. These parents may then feel even more pressure to prove they have done well for the child.

PHASE 4: THE ADOPTIVE FAMILY WITH A PRESCHOOL CHILD

When family members and the immediate social community may be informed of the child's adoptive status early on, there is a continued lifelong process of acknowledging the status with additional people as well as with the child himself. Parents whose children are racially different do not have to explain the obvious. Those whose children look as if they might be biological offspring struggle with whom, what, and when to tell about the adoption. The professional emphasis on openness has sometimes contributed to adoptive parents telling more people in more situations than was comfortable for them or even warranted. Under ordinary circumstances, when a stranger admires a child by saying something like, "Where did he get those beautiful blue eyes?" parents respond simply with pleasure. When such a comment is made about an adopted child, a parent may have an overdetermined need to explain that he is adopted, which in fact is irrelevant to the spirit of the question. Some parents have gone so far as to introduce their child as "our adopted" daughter or son in an effort to be as open as possible.

This constant referencing to the adoption applies a label that overstates the child's differentness. Bruno Bettelheim advised parents: "Acknowledge the difference but don't rub it in."[11] Most couples learn by trial and error in which circumstances it is appropriate and helpful to disclose information and which circumstances simply open them up to unnecessary discussion and troublesome comments or questions.

A commonly debated issue in the adoption literature is the question of how, what, and when to tell a child about his or her adoptive circumstances. In the 1930s adoption was kept a secret to protect everyone from possibly "immoral" facts. In the 1940s the "chosen child" approach was recommended by adoption agencies.[12] Child placement agencies and adoptive parents were encouraged to explain to adopted children that they were very special because their parents were able to choose them while biological parents simply had to take what was born to them. Some adults spun elaborate stories of going from crib to crib before they found their first choice. This approach was later discouraged as it became apparent that this effort to counteract feelings of abandonment in fact contributed to the children's fear that they could be "unchosen," that is, abandoned again. In the 1960s the prescription from the numerous adoption agencies then existing was to tell the child as early as possible in order to make the adoption concept a natural part of family life. Such advice is still common.[13]

Recent research on cognitive development of children reveals clear developmental changes in children's understanding of adoption. Brodzinsky and associates found that preschool c dren (adopted or not) demonstrate virtually no understanding of adoptive kinship structures.[14] Seven- to eight-year-olds demonstrate knowledge of the essential distinction between adoptive and biological parenthood, including its mediation by a non-family person or agency and manifest the conjecture that the biological parents may at any time reclaim the adopted child. Older children (ages 8 to 11) more strongly appreciate the unlikelihood of the biological parent actually reappearing. Finally, young adolescents demonstrate a stable conception of adoption as a permanent, legally encased structure. In a study that compared the conceptions of family relationships in unadopted kindergarten, second-grade, and fifth-grade children. Pickar made comparable observations.[15] He observed stages over which the child's cognitive comprehension of family and kinship structures progressively advanced toward the eventual distinction between blood ties and non-blood ties such as adoption.

These systematic data augment the conventional wisdom that suggests that children are incapable of comprehending the concept of adoption until age six or seven and that younger children, with their immature thinking processes, inevitably distort information they may have been given about their origins. The risk of this distortion when disclosure occurs at an early age must be weighed against the risk that the child will learn of his adoption from people other than his or her parents or at an age later than the child feels is fair, thus compromising feelings of trust in adoptive parents.

There is agreement in the literature that children should definitely be told of their adoption and that they should be told by their parents early enough so that they are most unlikely to hear it from others. How and what to tell remain questions for parents, who must rely on their own intuition and understanding of their own particular child, with sensitivity to his or her personality and stage of development. Such disclosure is one of the most difficult issues that plague adoptive parents. This may feel like the ultimate test of their parenting and/or the permanency of the rela-
ip ("Will he still love us if he knows?"). Almost all adoptive
wonder, "When should we tell and what should we
owever disconcerting, the fact is that no one—no grand-
o adoption expert, no good friend—has the answer to
stions.

circumstances arise before the age of adequate cogni-
ght force a parent to lie outright as an alternative to

telling a truth that may cause confusion. Children observe their friends' mothers' pregnancies and new babies; kindergartners talk about "where babies come from"; the family itself may adopt a new child or may have biological children before or after the adoption. Some children have little innate curiosity and may ask little about their origins before they are seven or eight. Others may be more curious and persistent in their questioning. A child of a different race may ask why she is not the same color. If a child says, "Susie's baby sister came from her mommy's tummy; did I come from your tummy?" a parent is hard-pressed not to answer honestly. Here an adoptive parent trades off an investment in trust for whatever confusions the information itself engenders. So adoptive parents hear the recommendations of "not too young and not too old" as the state of the art. There are other commonsense guidelines offered, such as choosing a neutral time and never making disclosure as a part of punishment or at an unhappy time for the family.

An additional complication exists when there are both biological and adopted children in the family. It is hard enough to experience unrealized wishes. It is even harder to see someone else have what you wish for. To compensate, adoptive parents sometimes bend over backward and revert to elevating adoption to a special "chosen child" status. This contributes to further tension between the children regarding their status in the family. It is likely to be more helpful to present adoptive or biological origins as facts of the family's life. Related feelings—on all sides—will need to be dealt with over time.

Ultimately, adoptive parents must use their own judgment on the basis of their understanding of themselves and their own particular child. It needs to be emphasized, however, that no matter how positive the circumstances may be or how sensitively the information is presented, hearing that one is adopted is not welcome news. Children react immediately in many different ways. Some cling to the positive message of being so wanted by the adoptive parents and "forget" for the time being that being wanted also means being unwanted by birth parents. Others are sad, angry, or uncomprehending. Factors such as age, gender, personality, and family dynamics will affect how the child begins to process this information.

Most parents wish they never had to tell. A very empathic father said, "If I could miraculously know that he would never find out from anyone else, I wouldn't tell him. I can imagine what it would feel like to hear such news—it makes my heart ache just to think about it. Unfortunately, there are no such miracles, and we will have to tell him." In most cases, the parents' worst fear—that they will not be loved or wanted as parents—is allayed. Parents and their extended family have confronted the lack of the bloodline in preparing for the adoption. The disclosure is the beginning of a new task, that of negotiating its meaning between parent and child, a process that will continue for a lifetime.

PHASE 5: THE ADOPTIVE FAMILY WITH A SCHOOL-AGE CHILD

As children enter school, their world as well as that of their family expands. There are new adults and new children who become important to them and influence them. These people all have their own thoughts and feelings about what it means to be adopted. Other children may "accuse" the child of having a stepmother rather than a "real" mother. School lessons about "where babies come from" may stir up uncomfortable feelings for children, who then may bring these feelings home to their parents. A very expressive and articulate seven-year-old adopted boy came home from school one day after baby chicks and been hatched in the classroom. He cuddled up next to his mother on the couch and said, "I wish I had been born from your tummy. How about if I sit on your lap and then pretend to get born from you. From now on we can say I was." The mother felt completely unprepared for such a request. She told him she wished she had given birth to him, too, but they both had to accept that it just did not happen that way. As she held him, she told him how glad she was, and would always be, that he had come to them, even through another woman's body. They shared a moment of warm empathy, which could not have occurred if this mother had not been able to acknowledge her own and her son's wishes.

School personnel and others may be insensitive to children's concrete use of language. Remarks about a child being "given away," "put up" for adoption, or lucky to have been "taken in" by the adoptive parents can cause some children great distress. "Mom, when you get 'put up' for adoption, where do they put you—on a shelf or something?" asked one little girl. Parents need to decide whom to inform and how to deal with adoption-related issues that emerge through the stimulation of the expanded environment.

The period of elementary school attendance is a time when

adopted children become able to conceptualize biological and adoptive relationships and recognize they have two sets of parents. They begin to struggle with this reality, fantasizing about the birth parents and attempting to understand why and how all this happened. They begin to construct their own stories about good parents and bad parents, good children and bad children. This is a time of life when children—adopted or not—commonly fantasize the existence of other (better) parents from whom they were taken.

Adopted children must deal with the reality that they *have* other parents and that these parents, as far as they know, agreed to give them away. Their confused, mixed feelings often take the form of a derogation of both the adoptive and birth parents. There may be subtle or not so subtle remarks about the offerings of the household compared to others: "Donny gets more allowance and gets to stay up later, and his parents don't make him eat his dinner before he can have dessert"; "Susie's parents get her a new bike every year, and she's going to get a new car when she's 16." All children at times compare their parents unfavorably with others. Adopted children's complaints pose an extra burden to parents as they are often thinly disguised comparisons with the child's fantasized birth parents. While these fantasies may cover the range from scum of the earth to lordly princes and princesses, the criticisms and comparisons tend to trigger adoptive parents' earlier concerns about whether they are good enough and whether they are *really* accepted by their child. Again, there may be the fear that the child would choose the birth parents over them if given the opportunity.

Adoptive parents may go through other difficult times of being tested. Adopted children frequently have both a wish and a fear that they will be "returned." The wish is that the birth parents will want them (after all); the fear is that birth parents will kidnap them (back) and take them away from the family to which they are attached. They may also fear that since they were not good enough to be kept the first time, they may still not be good enough to be kept. To answer the question "Will I be returned?" the child may behave in an utterly horrendous manner. This being a *real* test, the child is likely to exhibit those behaviors he or she has learned from experience are truly unacceptable to the parents. This is not everyday childlike behavior that needs everyday correction or ordinary discipline. This is the "getting under your skin" kind of behavior that unnerves parents. The child thus is asking, "Will you still keep me, even when you can't stand me?"

This prompts parents to ask themselves the same question and stirs up old feelings and wishes to have the idealized biological child (with the fantasy that such a child surely would never behave this way). There may be some piece of truth in this belief because while no child would ever meet the ideal, a biological child would not have such an intense need to test the permanency of the relationship. When there actually are biological children in the family, testing behavior may take the form of appearing as different from those children as possible. These tests of adoptees ordinarily occur when they first figure out what it means to be adopted and at developmental stages such as puberty and adolescence when issues of identity, belonging, and separation emerge. They occur for older adoptees some time after the initial honeymoon period. We will discuss these in more detail in the next chapter.

Ordinarily, these tests of adoptees are transient. They ask their questions, get their answers, and go on to the next point at which they need reassurance. But some adoptive parents and children do not past this test. This is particularly so in those cases where a child has been traumatized by separation (prior to the adoption) and then becomes compelled to effect rejection and abandonment again and again through provocative behavior. He repeats the trauma in an effort to master it. In some cases a child will, in fact, require a more structured placement. This is a time when outside intervention, such as family counseling, may help both children and parents understand the process that is taking place.

Parents, biological and adoptive, also vary in their ability to accept their child and to form a permanent bond. If they insist consciously or unconsciously that the child meet the standard of their idealized child, they will have difficulty tolerating a child who deviates from this image. Thus, the child experiences the parents' constant disappointment, internalizes it, and is likely to behave in even more troublesome ways. Parents who have not resolved adoption issues sufficiently to have fully claimed their child may be compromised in their ability to discipline and set limits of their youngster. For example, if parents have not differentiated their infertility from their ability to parent, they may not feel confident in their authority. If they continue to long for a biological child and have not accepted the validity of psychological parenting, they will not be prepared to "go the extra mile" that proves their wholehearted permanent commitment to this child.

The combination of the child's provocative behavior and the parents' inconsistent limits sets in motion a vicious cycle that neither parent nor child is able to interrupt. Such was the case with the V. family. Robert had been adopted in infancy by parents who came from conservative homes where conformity and good behavior were highly valued. Robert could really be one of them only if he met these standards. In testing the permanency of the relationship at age 12, Robert adroitly selected behaviors he consciously and unconsciously knew would challenge the attachment. His provocative foul language, slovenly hygiene, and irresponsible behavior were beyond Mr. and Ms. V.'s tolerance. They were unable to work with such behavior in their home. It was thus necessary for Robert to be placed in a residential treatment center despite the fact that his behavior was not out of control.

Similar behaviors were presented by Donna, age 10. Like Robert, she made herself obnoxious. Her parents recognized the test she posed and were determined to pass it. They set firm limits and chose wise battles. In so doing they proved to Donna that they felt she was their daughter forever. A similar test occurred in later adolescence with higher stakes. Again, Donna's parents met the challenge. Now an adult, Donna enjoys a relaxed relationship with her parents; all remember the battles and share satisfaction in having gotten beyond them.

Whatever the dynamics, there is consistent evidence that adopted children, particularly adolescents, are overrepresented in residential treatment programs. These placements do not necessarily mean that there has been a permanent severing of the adoptive relationship. It does mean that the home living situation has been found untenable and that the family has found it necessary to live apart from each other for some period of time. The bloodline automatically binds biological parents with their children through the most disappointing times; the lack of this bloodline for adoptive parents and children leaves open the question of permanency, which needs answering on both sides many times in the life course. Each time it is answered positively, there is a deepening of the bond that transcends blood ties.

PHASE 6: THE ADOPTIVE FAMILY WITH AN ADOLESCENT

In western society the family with an adolescent is commonly seen as one struggling with the difficult task of flexing its boundaries to meet the adolescent's increasing need for independence and the formation of his or her own identity. For the adoptive family these tasks carry special burdens.

Adolescents are well known for asserting their need for increasing freedom and independence from the family. Parents of adolescents are also well known for finding it difficult to let go of the children they have held close and nurtured for so many years. Attachment is something adoptive families often had to work to achieve, overcoming the underlying uncertainty posed by the facts of the origin of the family structure. Separation looms as a threat and a fear: "Will our family maintain its non-blood attachment even when the childrearing days are over?" Is achieving independence equivalent to being well launched or to eviction and abandonment? These are questions that both child and parent may ask.

For adoptive parents the common behavior of adolescents to prefer to spend increasing amounts of time away from home or to attach to other adults may stir up old fears that their child would really prefer others, that is, the birth parents. Adoptive parents may be particularly sensitive to emotional distance, which can be experienced as abandonment and rejection. This is a time when insecurities in the basic attachment are likely to reemerge.

As adolescents struggle to separate, parents also observe their struggle to work out who they are and who they want to be as adults. This is typically the time of life when adolescents experiment with many identities and present varying personae to themselves and others. "I never know who's coming down for breakfast. Is this going to be a preppie day, a punk day, or a hippie day? I wish she'd figure out who she is in this life" said one mother of a teenage daughter. It is not uncommon for the emerging personae to reflect de-identification with parents—and often a thorough rejection of their lifestyle and values. While all parents of adolescents must brace for this onslaught—temporary though it may be—it poses an additional burden and threat to adoptive parents.

For adoptive adolescents the search for identity is complicated by the triadic family structure. This is a time when, consciously and unconsciously, adoptees assess their biological and psychological bonds and attempt to achieve an identity that is some combination of both. They may drastically change or shift identities back and forth between the child they were raised to be and the child they think they were born to be. "It's almost like Janie has a split personality," said one mother.

One day—or even one moment—she is this lovely, regular teen-ager who has her own life but is clearly a product of our family. She talks about carrying on family traditions and clearly values what she has with us all. When she is like this, I feel confident in her and her future. And then—for no apparent reason—she is almost another person. She talks like a street kid, dresses like a floozy, doesn't seem to care about anything or anybody. What is most frightening is that when she is in this state, she makes very bad decisions and I fear for her welfare. I'd like to think that the latter state is a "phase" and underneath it is really Janie. But to tell you the truth, they both seem like real parts of her. It's scaring me to death.

Janie's mom is right in perceiving the complicated nature of her identifications. Only with time will she be able to sort out who she is, as a product of both biology and upbringing.

Almost inevitably, at some point the long-anticipated, long-dreaded epithet "YOU'RE NOT MY REAL PARENTS" is certain to be hurled. It is usually followed by a few well-chosen remarks about what real (better) parents would or would not do. For years adoptive parents wonder how they would feel if their child ever said such a thing. A mother who had enjoyed a warm and easy relationship with her son was amazed at how little it troubled her when he hurled this accusation at her at age 14. "I knew I was as real as it gets, and I knew he knew it, too. I felt for him—in terms of what he was struggling with—but did not feel it had much to do with me as a person or as a mother." Others have felt deeply hurt and sometimes devastated by such charges. Whatever inse-curities, whatever regrets might exist about how good or real a parent one has been are called up at this time. Inside, one might be thinking, "You're right, I haven't been a really good father; you deserve someone better." Or there may instead be defensive rage: "I feel like I've given my heart and soul to you and you tell me I'm not your real mother. How dare you!" These are not easy times.

Part of the de-identification—that is, behaving as if not a mem-ber of this family—may be renewed testing behavior. "Are we still family if I am rude? How about if I am a slob? A slut? How about a delinquent? How about whatever I know you don't ap-prove of?" Once again, the test is *real*, and parents find them-selves really not liking or approving of their children. When bio-logical parents feel this way, they may regret they ever bore the child but are stuck with the fact that they did and will always be biologically related. Fertile parents who adopted may feel that their good intentions produced bad results, thus invalidating the social good. When adoptive parents experience these negative feelings, they may seek some comfort in remembering that they did not create this child, that they only made the "mistake" of adopting him. Surely, their own fantasized child would not behave in this manner. The viability of the bond is once again challenged.

The identity struggle and need to test may also involve a conscious or unconscious wish to search for the birth parents. Adolescents may express this wish in a provocative and punitive way in times of wrath, pushing their adoptive parents to the limit. Some may deny the wish out of fear of hurting their adoptive parents. They may or may not ask their parents' permission and help in the process. There are now many support groups offering help for the adoptee to search. Some parents may feel so threatened by the process that they may effect an estrangement with their child. Some will feel it as a necessary part of growing up. Others may experience mixed feelings, both threatened and empathic, and participate in whatever ways seem tolerable to them.

Some adoptees exhibit a kind of "wandering" behavior. They attach to other families and other adults, such as coaches and teachers, and seem to float from one to another. This behavior reflects the child's search. It is not unusual for adopted adolescents to attach to families where it appears that parents kept their children in spite of difficult circumstances, something their own birth parents did not do. Families where poverty, illness, single parenthood, or multigenerational interaction occurs may be idealized by the adopted adolescent. This often leaves adoptive parents feeling both confused and enraged at what appears to be an injustice in the face of all the resources they feel they have poured into their child. The urge to retaliate may or may not be controlled.

Sexual boundaries between parent and child and among siblings may also be challenged. While families establish their own rules regarding the nature of the expression of sexuality within the family, biological families rely on an incest taboo based on their biological relationship. As we know, this taboo is sometimes transgressed. Adoptive parents build their own taboos based on the need for these boundaries in family life. At such times when controlling impulsive urges is more difficult, family members may need to reinforce these sexual boundaries. Parents will need to remind each other to maintain privacy when dressing and to ensure that the bathroom or bedroom door is fully closed since children can be so easily overstimulated. Sometimes sexual attraction is handled by distancing through withdrawal or aggression. Adopted siblings without biological ties may at times need firm parental support in controlling the sexual attraction toward each other. For them there may need to be rules about privacy in bedrooms and bathrooms so that they can enjoy each other's company without the added burden of overstimulation.

These extra issues for the adoptive family can be highly inflammatory and can make life in the adolescent years a time of real crisis. Everyone involved needs to accept the existence and influence of both parental sets. This may be particularly difficult for adoptive parents, who may feel they are losing their child's loyalty, after all their daily efforts, as he or she assumes an adult identity.

What appears to cause so much anguish in the process is the way in which adolescent issues and adoption issues converge and become so intensified in parent–child relationships. Sometimes there are antagonistic needs. Parents may need reassurance that normal separation during adolescence does not mean abandonment and rejection whereas adopted adolescents may have a deep need to emancipate themselves from the adoptive family in order to make room to explore other parts of themselves. Adoptive parents need to learn to support healthy independent strivings without feeling abandoned. They must come to recognize their adolescent's interest in his or her birth family as a natural developmental step, in most cases, rather than an act of disloyalty or evidence of a lack of appreciation for the real psychological relationship. Adoptive parents face the formidable task of maintaining faith in the real relationship they have established with the child while they watch him or her appear to reject or disregard its value.

As adoptive parents and their children struggle with these issues independently and interactively, they lay the groundwork for establishing a new, mutually agreed-upon contract in which parents and children accept their family's adoptive status. This new contract can take place only when both parents and adolescent have afforded themselves and the other the opportunity to look openly at the triadic family system and accept it as a part of their ongoing lives.

PHASE 7: THE ADOPTIVE FAMILY
WITH A YOUNG ADULT

The launching of children requires families to face and deal with numerous entrances and exits that all carry significant emotional push and pull. The grieving related to initial leavings can be replaced by feelings of being intruded upon and then again abandoned as young adults gradually shift the place they call home. In an essay entitled "Launching Children and Moving On" Paulina McCullough speaks of the ebb and flow of family dynamics during this phase.[16] She describes a transitory ebb with the launching of children followed by "the creation of a new state of relatedness when the offspring begin courting and subsequently marrying."[17] She goes on to state that "the degree of success that the parents have demonstrated in dealing with issues of autonomy, responsibility and connectedness with their respective families of origin will have definitive impact on their success in handling these issues with their grown children."[18]

Once again the process is even more complicated for adoptive families. Certainly, parents' own histories of leaving home have a major impact on how they experience and deal with their own children's departures. But in adoptive families arrivals and leavings have additional meanings. These children did not arrive in the usual way; it makes sense that they also will not leave in the usual way. Arranging for their arrival was so difficult that some parents may always feel they are living on "borrowed time" with a "borrowed child." Perhaps the belief that they can have them forever seems too good to be true. When Melissa B. graduated from college, her mother found herself bereft. Despite having enjoyed a warm and close relationship with her daughter, she feared that Melissa might no longer want her. "I know all kids have to go off on their own," she said, "and Melissa should too. In some ways I feel I deserved her as long as I was taking care of her. Maybe I don't deserve her anymore." It was not until she experienced Melissa's continued attachment that this anxiety abated.

How well adoptive parents and children were able to resolve the independence and abandonment issues that emerged during the adolescent years will have a bearing on how difficult a shift the transition to adulthood is likely to be. Are parent and child still shaky with each other? Are they still questioning whether there can be a reasonable adult–adult relationship in later years? When rebellious adolescent behavior subsides, there can be a reaffirmation of ties within the adoptive family. The adoptee will always struggle with the integration of identities, but entrance into adulthood diminishes adoptive parents' control. Diminishing external pressures thereby allow for focus on internal pressures; adoptees thus tend to begin fighting more within themselves than with parents. Parents may still be distressed at the forms of identification adopted and the nature of decisions made but are likely to see more evidence of their child's tie to the family. The child's cameo appearances on holidays, common in the adolescent years, may begin to be replaced by real visits and a renewed appreciation of the family's values and traditions. Absences may no longer carry with them the sting of disloyalty or rejection. While we have no studies comparing the launching phases of adoptive families with that of nonadoptive families, the complicated and intense nature of separation issues suggests that it may take longer for adoptive families to complete the tasks involved. There may, in fact, be more entrances and exits as the family works at these tasks, completing them at a later date than might occur in the nonadoptive family. A later launching, therefore, may be quite normal in the adoptive family.

As adopted people begin searching for mates, they are likely to have more interest and curiosity about their own genealogy. Nevertheless, adoptive parents may not be able to answer important questions. Potential mates and their families may have concerns about the adopted one's hereditary base and may express similar interest. There may be a kind of revisiting of the extended family issues that confronted the parents when they first prepared to adopt. This new part of the family may need to confront their own fears and biases regarding the missing genealogical link between themselves and the next generation. How much does the unknown matter to them? While this phenomenon is probably rare, one girl of a "well-bred" family broke off a serious relationship when she learned her boyfriend was adopted and thus without a known pedigree. The boy came from a very high functioning adoptive family in which he had a strong, secure relationship. They were all stunned by this kind of rejection.

As adoptive parents begin thinking about what they have to hand down to the next generation, they may wonder which experiences of their home life their children will want to carry on. Looking forward to the future, parents may once again need to revisit their past fantasies. Perhaps the idealized biological child was the spitting image of his dad, the son who was to work by his father's side and carry on the family business; there may be reemerging pangs of disappointment and a feeling that a family tradition has ended when an adopted child makes choices that are extremely different from the family business. The difficulty here is the imposition of a parent's wish on a child—adopted or biological—who does not share it. This imposition denies the adoptee's status as a real, living part of the family history. Here, in the continuing process, is yet another level of integration of genetics and upbringing. Adoptive parents as well as their children must come to see that this new adult, this whole person—a combination of both heredity and environment—is what provides continuity to the family. The integration at this time is a strong basis for the establishment of a new contract between parents and child, with all parties feeling the strength of the ongoing bond that is based on life experience with each other and also accepting the triadic family.

Adoptees who reproduce enter into an experience of which their adoptive parents were deprived. The circumstances may stir up varied and conflictual feelings. On the one hand, adoptive parents may be delighted to become grandparents. Creating a family was not easy for them to do and, more likely than not, the couple did not achieve the family size they would have liked. Having the opportunity to expand the family generationally might seem very appealing: "I always wanted a houseful of children and had to settle for only two. Now, maybe—at least at times—I'll have a houseful of grandchildren," dreamed one mother. "I love the idea of having our family live on."

On the other hand, adoptive parents may revisit old, painful realities that caused them sadness and anger. They may experience envy of their own children as well as inadequacy in being unable to offer the kind of counsel and empathy a person who has experienced childbirth is able to offer: "I feel terrible that I can't give her any advice about hemorrhoids or swollen ankles or contractions. I've always felt really competent as a mother and now feel at a loss about being able to help—or even empathize—in such an important event in her life. I hate it that she has to call her mother-in-law for help on these matters." Adoptive parents may also experience moments of renewed grief and bitterness at what was denied them. One adoptive mother was so ashamed of her infertility that she was still denying adoption: "Breast-feeding never came easy to me," she told her daughter when her daughter gave birth. Like any other life transition, birth of a grandchild is an opportunity for mastery for adoptive parents. While they may not have gone through a pregnancy and delivery themselves, they have had the opportunity to learn from others' experiences and can offer this learning to their own children. One adoptive mother stayed with her daughter in the hospital and for the first 10 days at home following the birth of her first grandchild. She found herself reading and asking everything she could about breast-feeding and postnatal care. In this way she ably informed and supported the new mother through experiences she herself had never had. As adoptive parents watch their children attach to what is their first known blood relative, there may be a resurgence of the insecurity of the non-blood tie: "Will she attach to the child and forget me? Will I be too envious of her ability to procreate to really be able to enjoy it for her and with her?" Once again, work needs to be done to acknowledge these feelings and deal with them in a way that allows for a continued relationship and for the pleasures of grandparenthood. Adoptive parents again have to separate the issues of infertility and competence to parent—and now to grandparent. Not having given birth to a child does not mean they cannot learn about such an experience and support their children as they become biological parents, but more important than guiding them through the physiological changes of pregnancy and childbirth, they can offer themselves as examples of loving mothers and fathers.

PHASE 8: THE ADOPTIVE FAMILY IN LATER LIFE

Becoming part of the older generation involves many changes in life circumstances that require adaptation. There is a shift to becoming elders in the family where the children are now the adults. There may be declining health, loss of a spouse, loss of peers, grandparenthood, job retirement, and financial strain. There are renewed issues about dependency as elders may truly need the help of others—including their children—to manage current life challenges. In the process of dealing with these challenges there is a confrontation with the issue of mortality and the difficult task of reviewing one's life.

With an increasing population of elderly people we have become more aware of the difficulties families face in providing proper support and caregiving when these are necessary. Adult children in the middle generation often find themselves taking care of children and parents at the same time. Dual-career families are even more strained in terms of available time and energy. Geographic separation makes frequent visits and attention impractical. The saying "One mother can take care of five children, but five children can't take care of one mother" is increasingly true. In adoptive families the shift may be even more complicated, depending on how well issues of dependency and independence were resolved in earlier life phases.

Parents, by nature and by their own family-of-origin experiences may be resistant or reluctant to ask for or receive help from their children. Adoptive parents may be even more reluctant if they do not feel the kind of bond that entitles them to their children's ongoing caregiving. A vicious cycle can result, with parents not asking for help because they feel the children do not want or should not want to give it and children not responding because they have not been asked to, which, in turn, leaves parents feeling disappointed but justified in their beliefs. This behavior is consistent with the borrowed time–borrowed children theme that is sometimes part of the belief system of adoptive parents, a conviction that denies those who have not resolved it the experience of a close lifelong relationship with their children.

The later years call up issues of mortality and the legacy left behind. Adoptive parents must confront the lack of biological progeny and whatever that means to them. There may be moments of grieving in the recognition that there will be no biological descendants to carry on and renewed wishes for the fantasized biological child who would fill that function.

OUTCOME FOR ADOPTIVE PARENTS

While there are extensive references to adoptive parents throughout the literature, there are few works that directly address the adoptive parent experience over time. Thus, there is little data from which to make an assessment of outcome. Nevertheless, there has been a tendency for writers to quote from the small number of case studies in presenting the "characteristics of adoptive parents."

Like other alternative families, such as single-parent, remarried, or those headed by gay parents, adoptive families must struggle with their ambiguity and unorthodoxy and come to define what is adaptive in their own formation and functioning. David Kirk studied adoptive parents in terms of their tendency to deny or acknowledge differences between their family and biological families.[19] These ideas have more recently been refined by Brodzinsky, who expands the conceptual range from "rejection of difference" through "acknowledgment of differences" to "insistence on differences."[20] He observes that adoptive parents cope by traveling throughout this range at different stages in their children's developments. For example, parents may deny differences during infancy while they bond with the baby, and an "insistence on differences" may occur during a stormy adolescence when parents find "owning" this child difficult. Some adoptive parents may exhibit little flexibility and may remain entrenched in one attitudinal state, thus denying themselves more flexible coping mechanisms.

There have not been large surveys of adoptive parents or significant efforts to study their ongoing adjustment, as there have been for birth parents and for adoptees. The lack of this attention to these members of the adoption circle is an interesting issue in itself, suggesting a lack of concern for these participants, perhaps assuming that their needs are most fully met by the arrangement of an adoption.

CONCLUSION

When an individual or a couple decides to adopt a child, they hope that this option will serve them better than the alternatives of remaining childless or limiting the size of their family. Some fertile adopters hope to enhance their family life while meeting a social need.

Significant factors that contribute to a successful adoptive parenting experience are the quality of the preparation for adopting and the ability to deal with the special challenges inherent in adoptive relationships. In preparing for adoption, parents need to take time to examine their motivations and sufficiently clear away agenda that will interfere with this new attachment. They need to understand for example, that adoptees do not cure infertility or prove anyone is a good person or parent. These kinds of issues need to be sufficiently resolved so that the child enters the family without impossible burdens. There will, of course, be influences on the adoptive parents from the past—as there are for all parents—that will affect the parenting experience. The special developmental tasks discussed in this chapter are in addition to the maturational achievements required of any parent.

The factor most important in coping with the sometimes formidable developmental tasks is an acceptance of these tasks as a normal and necessary part of adoptive parenting. Coming to terms with this normality includes acceptance of the wish that life could have been different, that life could have been without the stresses that are an inevitable part of the adoptive family process. Successful coping involves noting these real feelings and then moving on to dealing with the realities. Most adoptive parents wish they had given birth to their children and wish they did not have to deliver to them the painful news of their relinquishment by their biological parents. They nonetheless do what they have to do in the best way they know. This *is* their life, and they have the opportunity to experience gratification both in the intimacy of the relationships and in their ability to master these special tasks.

There may be times when adoptive parents have concerns about themselves or their children that they find difficult to handle themselves. They may turn to adoptive parent groups or post-adoption counselors for needed clarification and support. When they continue to be distressed by their own feelings and functioning or by disturbance in their relationship with their child, it is time to seek therapeutic help. Sometimes the parents' work with a therapist will be sufficient to achieve the family's goals; sometimes treatment will include the children as well. Parents should be careful to choose a therapist who is experienced and informed in issues of adoption (see chapter 6).

The success of the experience of being an adoptive parent can be measured only in contrast to its alternatives—childlessness or life without this child in their family. There may be instances where adoptive parents feel that the challenge of a particular child or adoption in general was too great for them and they regret having taken it on. Most often, however, there is a recognition of the enrichment of life through the loving and raising of children—adopted or not—and a feeling of competence at having mastered the necessary tasks. One's legacy lives in a child who carries the memories, experiences, and heirlooms—both material and psychological—of the adoptive family.

CHAPTER 4

GROWING UP ADOPTED

Developmental Tasks of Adoptees

BIBLICAL AND CLASSICAL LITERATURE OFFER many representations of the plight of adopted children. Moses was left in the bulrushes, Oedipus was abandoned and adopted, and Joseph was sold by his family of origin. The experiences of relinquished or abandoned children are also dramatized in children's literature, such as the stories of Hansel and Gretel and the beloved Babar.

Historical and current data indicate that children in need of permanent adoptive homes come from a wide range of classes, cultures, religions, national origins, and personal circumstances. Many such children are adopted informally within their extended families; others require placement with nonrelatives. Nonrelative adoptions have been most common in cases where the child was conceived outside of marriage either in a culture where this circumstance carries a social stigma or in a family that is unwilling or unable to provide adequate care for a child. The majority of these children are relinquished in infancy; those who are relinquished when older have often had multiple placements in foster care or in institutions.

Most children now in adoptive homes and most adult adoptees were placed as infants following the mode of confidential adoption. Their birth parents relinquished parental rights, and their adoptive parents welcomed them. Little information was shared between the two sets of parents.

Let us look now at the actual development of these children and the issues they face. We will look primarily at children placed at infancy, but we will note the similarities and differences between their experiences and those of older or multiply placed children.

PHASE 1: CIRCUMSTANCES OF CONCEPTION, PREGNANCY, AND BIRTH

In the best of all worlds, the birth of a child is planned and happily anticipated. Not only are these the most favorable circumstances for parents but it provides a sense of comfort and validation to children to know that their parents wanted them and made active efforts at producing them. These circumstances contribute to a child's positive autobiographical sense of himself as having entered the world with a legitimate place and birthright.

In contrast, the first piece of autobiographical data for most adopted children is that they were a mistake, a person who was not planned and not meant to be. This circumstance is not unique to adoptees. Nonadoptees whose conceptions were unplanned often question their legitimacy in terms of their right to be. Even the unplanned but welcome child may have some sense of being extra or unnecessary or a burden in some basic way. A child of the undesired gender may always feel that he or she is not "right" and may try to compensate by developing characteristics of the other gender to be more gratifying to one or both parents and thus earn a more legitimate place. For example, it is not uncommon for one of an all-female sibling group to develop into a tomboy to meet a parent's wishes for a son.

For adoptees, the relinquishment by their birth parents certifies their being a problem; they are people whose very being caused a problem, one that was solved by extrusion. This is the fact, however it may later be explained or rationalized. Other facts around their conception may also have impact on the way adoptees feel about themselves. It may matter to them whether they were born out of a loving relationship, a casual relationship, or a relationship of violence. It may matter whether their parents were married to each other or not, or married to others. It may matter whether they perceive their birth parents to have been irresponsible regarding birth control, victims of a real accident, or simply unable to care for them.

These facts surrounding conception tend to contribute to a primal sense of the self, and adoptees can organize them in an infinite number of combinations as they make up autobiographical stories that may have little or no resemblance to what they have been told. For example, a 7-year-old girl had been told that her parents had been too young to get married and raise a child and wanted her to have a good home with both a mom and a dad. They arranged for her adoption through the social worker at the family agency. The child's retelling included some embellishment reflecting her feelings about the event: she reported that her parents were too young to raise children but her mother still wanted to keep her though her father said she could not. Her father made her mother put her in a box on the doorstep even though her mother cried and cried and begged to keep her. Finally, the social worker came in her van and picked her up and put her in the back with all the other babies she had picked up that day. She took them all to their adoptive homes.

It was clearly important to this child to feel that her mother gave her away only when forced to do so. There are likely to be other versions of this story from her as she grows and develops. These initial "facts" will require confrontation and processing throughout her life.

Other basic facts of an adoptee's life are, as for all people, the realities of their biological base. Biological factors have only recently been studied systematically and were previously overlooked as significant factors in the development of adoptees. Prior to these studies in the adoption field, children were viewed as a kind of tabula rasa for whose development adoptive parents bore full responsibility. Studies since the mid-1960s indicate that there are significant genetic factors in human development, some of which seem highly impervious to environmental influences. These early studies suggest that genetics plays a significant role in intelligence, certain major mental illnesses, antisocial personality disorders, substance abuse, and attention deficit disorders.[1] It is possible that in some cases the traits of these disturbances in birth parents may be related to the occurrence of the unplanned pregnancy and relinquishment. For example, a woman who has difficulty with impulse control may find herself pregnant and unable to care for her child. But it is important to note that this information about genetic influence does not mean we should conclude that adoptees, in fact, come from a more risky genetic pool. We simply have no way of comparing the relinquishing parent's genetic base to that of other single parents or, for that matter, to the parental population at large.

Adopted children may or may not ever be given much information about their heredity and may have to rely primarily on what they observe about themselves that they attribute to heredity. Most adoptive parents are given only shards of information about their child's birth parents. Once again, children tend to draw their own conclusions; they may feel absolutely certain that their birth mother or father has exactly the same shade of hair or eyes, is just as fat or thin, just as smart or dumb as they see themselves to be. They may forever wonder whether mental and physical illnesses, personality characteristics, and developmental course are genetically based. While the question of nature versus nurture remains an ambiguous one in general, it may be more problematic for adoptees who are deprived of basic information and thus must rely on fantasy and conjecture to attempt to sort out these aspects of their being. Adopted children who live with or know their biological parents also assess their genetic roots and wonder if the problems that made their parents unable to raise them are part of their constitution as well. There will be many phases in which adoptees attempt to sort out the hereditary and environmental factors relevant to their lives.

It is now common knowledge that the fetus is affected by the mother's behavior. Low birth weights and other physical anomalies have been proven to be caused by poor nutrition, smoking, and alcohol and drug use during pregnancy. It is less clear how a mother's emotions affect the fetus.

Social scientists who study infant attachment tell us that bonding between mother and baby begins in utero as the mother and child experience each other's being. No one knows specifically what the effect of that experience is but it is commonly believed that the prenatal environment of a happy, relaxed, well-cared-for mother is more conducive to the birth of a healthy baby than is that of a stressed, depressed mother who receives poor medical care. The prenatal experience for all babies varies along this continuum; a feature that is unique to the adoptee is that the birth mother consciously and unconsciously experiences anticipatory grief during her pregnancy. This is a difficult quality to measure, and we have little data on what impact this may have on the fetus. Some relinquishing mothers may effectively deny the loss during pregnancy and relate to the fetus emotionally and physically as if all were well. Others may subjectively experience intense feelings of anxiety and depression. The most reasonable inference would be that the circumstances of the pregnancy of a relinquishing mother make it more difficult for her to provide a positive physical and emotional prenatal environment for her baby and place these babies at greater risk. Biology cannot yet determine how sensitive any particular fetus is to the environment and what degree of impact, if any, it may have on him.

PHASE 2: THE POSTPARTUM PERIOD

Adopted children have a wide range of preadoption experiences. One that all have in common is having been physically and emotionally separated from their birth mothers. We know from observing infants in general that there are differences in the intensity of their earliest attachments. Some need constant closeness and attention from mothers while others appear quite self-content and easily satisfied by other caretakers. The degree of trauma, therefore, of being separated from the familiar—the sounds, movements, temperature, smells of the mother—will vary among adoptees. How well they recover will depend on their own temperament and the quality of the environment in which they are placed. Some children experience multiple placements before they reach their adoptive home. It is not uncommon for there to be some time in the hospital and one or more foster home placements prior to a permanent adoption. Each of these moves can exacerbate an already prenatally stressed and natally traumatized child. It may be that some children who are loaded in the negative direction with genetic vulnerability, prenatal stress, and natal trauma may forever carry with them a vulnerability that even the most favorable adoptive circumstances could not completely alleviate. They may experience a kind of primal wound that just won't heal. At the other extreme, a genetically less vulnerable fetus may weather prenatal stress and the separation from its mother quite easily, thus requiring the new environment only to be "good enough," rather than therapeutic. Most children fall somewhere between these two extremes. What can be said of their commonality is that they have all suffered from maternal loss and are in need of a consistent, nurturing environment to help them recover.

PHASE 3: INFANCY

Given these preadoption circumstances, infants will enter their adoptive homes in varying states of well-being and with their own particular temperaments. They will be met by families with their own varying states of well-being and their own strengths and weaknesses in dealing with their child's needs. This match is a crucial one on both a temporary and a long-term basis.

All parents have stories of their first experiences with their infants. These stories become part of family lore:

> "He was a wise old man from day one."
> "She was born sucking and has never been able to get enough."
> "She was solid as a rock—sure of herself."
> "He wouldn't let me near him—wouldn't snuggle—wanted to be left alone."
> "She arrived with open arms, ready to love and be loved."

Some parents report significant changes in these traits with time; many others say their child remained the same. These stories are reflections of the "match"—the way the child presented himself or herself and the way that presentation was received. For example, the baby described as "wanting to be left alone" could be experienced as anything from "admirably independent" through "needing to be gently coaxed into warming up" to "aloof and rejecting." These perceptions will have impact on the kinds of interactions offered to adopted children and, to some degree, on the way the children come to perceive themselves. Thus, both the adoptee and the parents must first recover from their traumas before they, as unfettered selves, are open to bonding. When parents have made significant progress in healing the wounds of their reproductive problems, they are in a better position to help their children with their tasks. Fertile or not, parents still seriously struggling with their own issues regarding the decision to adopt may be much less able to accept the child as he or she is and to offer the kind of help the child needs in entering the family.

The process of integration and matching will be more difficult in some circumstances than others. A critical factor is the degree to which adoptive parents have been able to achieve realistic expectations about the adoption process. If they have accepted the fact that adoption is not just the same as biological parenting but may present added stresses, they will be best prepared to accept the child as he or she is. A difficult match occurs when a couple, not having come to terms with their own infertility, are looking for the equivalent of their idealized biological child and instead are faced with a traumatized, troubled child. There is a similarly poor match when fertile couples seek an idealized child of a particular gender or, wishing to rescue a needful child, find themselves with one who doesn't respond in a way that allows them to feel effective in their rescuing efforts. The easiest match is between a couple who are realistic about the special needs of the adopted child and a child who is highly responsive to their efforts. In fact, parents who have accepted that adopting may present special challenges are best equipped to help any child with this early stage of adjustment.

As adopted babies experience everyday life in their new home, they develop a new familiarity with the predictability and continuity of the household. Each added day of this sameness contributes to a security that continues to heal the original trauma and lends promise to the need not to be retraumatized. Through this comfort, adopted babies develop trust in their caretakers and in themselves. One father reported, ''She was a wreck when we brought her home. It took weeks before she settled down and was able to eat and sleep in a comfortable way. It was months before she was calm enough to even notice we were there.'' Over time, each family will make its own adjustments, and there will be sufficient recovery to allow for bonding to develop and for a new real family to begin.

PHASE 4: PRESCHOOL YEARS

Children never seem to wait too long before they move from a mastered stage to a new one, often leaving parents in their wake. Attached, cuddly infants all too quickly become striving, demanding toddlers with the urge to make their own choices and exert control. The parents' ability to accept these aspects of their child's development contributes to furthering the child's self-esteem. Similarly, behaviors reflecting sexuality and aggression are tests of the parent–child relationship. If adoptive parents have major concerns regarding their child's inheritance of the birth parents' lack of control of sexuality and aggression, they may misunderstand and misinterpret their child's normal behavioral development. When these behaviors are responded to for just what they are, there is support for the child's healthy initiative and a strengthening of the parent–child tie.

Sometimes parents choose the preschool period as a time to disclose the child's adoptive status to him or her. Using the word *adopted* in a natural way as early as possible was the recommendation of child welfare workers throughout the 1970s, and many still make such a recommendation. As previously mentioned, more recent research has indicated that children under the age of 6 or 7 lack the capacity to understand the concepts of adoptive and biological parenthood. Children of this age think in a concrete and magical way. The concreteness is reflected in the literal way they process language. For example, a 3-year-old who answered the phone was asked what he was doing and replied, "I am talking to you." A 4-year-old who overheard a parent say, "Keep an eye out for the squirrel" was quiet and confused and then asked, "Are you really going to take your eye out, Dad?"

With their process of magical thinking, which Selma Fraiberg wrote about so beautifully in *The Magic Years*, youngsters magically make one thing into another.[2] In their minds, a wish or a fear can instantaneously become a reality. A child who wanted to kill off a baby brother who later dies firmly believes that his wishes caused the death. Wishing Dad would go away becomes absolutely causal in the child's mind when father leaves the home after a divorce. The inalterable firmness with which children maintain these beliefs despite adults' efforts at clarification and reassurance impresses us with the power of this phenomenon.

News of the adoption at this stage, then, paves the way for confusion and allows the child to come to his own concrete and magical conclusions regarding the adoption. One 3-year-old named Jason visited a friend's new baby sister. There was some discussion of where babies come from. Back home again, Jason asked if he had come from his mommy's tummy the way his friend Becky's sister had been born. His adoptive mother explained that the lady that had made him couldn't take care of him so she brought him to Family Services where they found good homes for children who needed them. She warmly told him of how happy they were to have him come home to them. The next time they were out in the car, his parents drove by the agency and pointed out the building in which they had received him, tenderly describing what a happy day it had been. Several months later, the parents overheard a conversation Jason was having with his friend Becky. He explained to her that while her sister had come from her mommy's tummy, he himself had come from a building downtown; he was born from the family building. Neither Becky nor Jason seemed clear about which sort of birth was better.

In the course of the disclosure of her adoption, 5-year-old Susan was told she had been "put up" for adoption. In her household things that were "put up" were items like candy and matches, whatever was meant to be kept out of reach. She confused her mother one day when she asked how the social workers get the babies down from the shelves to be adopted. To her, putting them up on shelves in the first place seemed like a very strange thing to do with a baby.

One fair-haired 4-year-old whose parents had dark hair was frequently asked where he got his blond hair. His well-intentioned parents, following guidelines to be open about adoption as early as possible, frequently explained that it was because he was adopted. Public responses ranged from "Isn't he lucky!" to "Aren't you lucky!" The child perceived that there was something different (and maybe not so good) about being "'dopted." The parents later learned that he, in his 4-year-old mode of thinking, decided that all blond people were adopted and that there was something different and not so good about all of them that required luck to make it right. Other children latch on to the notion of being special in some way. But "special" is also different and defies children's basically conforming nature and wish to be "regular." In families where there are both biological and adopted children, there is an ongoing process of sorting out what is "regular" and what is "special" and trying to determine which is better. Each child may feel the other to be more valued by the parents at different times.

The content, quality, circumstances, and timing of the disclosure of the adoption will interact with the child's developmental state. When disclosure occurs during the preschool stage, children will subject the information to their concrete and magical mode of thinking and make sense of it in any way they can. Some interactions are more debilitating than others. Disclosure at this stage is a trade-off of trust over comprehension. Processing this news is a developmental task directly related to age and cognitive maturity. Parents can be sensitive to the possible confusions and make efforts at clarification. The confusions are not necessarily damaging, and most will fall into the category of "what I used to think," that is, erroneous, often illogical, beliefs that naturally become clarified in time.

PHASE 5: SCHOOL YEARS

As children reach school age, they make significant shifts in their cognitive abilities and are able to understand some concepts previously beyond them. The noted developmental psychologist Piaget speaks of this as the emergence of "operational" functions. Through both physical maturation and experience, the child becomes increasingly able to understand causal relationships and think planfully and logically.[3] If children have been told of their adoption earlier, they will now begin to rework this information and their prior conclusions. There may continue to be vestiges of these earlier themes or beliefs as well as the feelings associated with them. The child who thought she had been put up on a shelf may maintain some sense of being "off-limits." The blond-haired boy may always feel that his hair makes him unusual in some way.

If told of adoption during the school-age phase, children are able to understand that they have two sets of parents, one biological and one adoptive. The news upsets a basic belief in the inviolability of the parent–child tie. Ironically, a secure attachment to adoptive parents makes the news of relinquishment even more difficult to understand. An adoptee might think, "If parents are attached to their children the way my adoptive parents are attached to me, how can it be that parents would give a child away? Everything was fine. Why would they tell me something like this and make it all so confusing?" For the child, some basic tenets of human nature and sense of well-being are disrupted. Some children become noticeably distressed at the news and reflect this distress emotionally and behaviorally. Some muster immediate defenses, convincing themselves that being adopted is as good as or better than not being so. In all cases the news is recognized as significant, and the children begin the process of making their own sense of it.

In a child's manner of thinking, if something bad happens it must be somebody's fault. Adopted children begin to struggle with feelings about the whole cast of characters in the adoption circle, including themselves. They experience mixed feelings toward each set of parents and toward themselves. Sometimes they split these feelings by making one party good and the other bad, either consistently or alternately. Other players in the adoption drama may also be implicated: doctors, lawyers, and social workers may be seen as the ones who did good or bad deeds, thus protecting the primary characters. A child may ponder the nature and motives of everyone involved: "Was the birth mother a good mother who gave a bad baby away, or was I a good baby and she a (very) bad mother? Maybe she was good and I was good and my adoptive parents were bad in stealing me from her. Maybe somebody else stole me from her and sold me to them. Some days I think I was bad; some days I think those other people were bad."

School-age years are a time when all children have fantasies about their origins. Now they are beyond the immature stage of seeing their parents as all-knowing and all-powerful. As they mature, they experience daily disappointments in these previously all-powerful parental figures. They recognize mistakes their parents make and sometimes see them not measuring up to other parents they know. The same parents who were once able to make a hurt "all better" with a kiss sometimes now even willfully contribute to their frustration and pain. In an attempt to find some equilibrium in the face of these observations, many children, adopted or not, develop a "family romance" in which they fantasize that they are not, in fact, the offspring of these less than perfect people but were instead born of noble parents—beautiful, wonderful princes and princesses—and somehow ended up with these plain folks. There are many versions of the circumstances through which children imagine they were shifted from their noble parents to the ones they live with. In some versions they were forcibly removed; in others, the perfect parents died or were somehow otherwise lost to them. The common thread is the loss of the perfect parents and the harsh reality of life with the not nearly perfect ones. This fantasy provides respite from life's daily disappointments and makes them more tolerable.

For adopted children these romantic fantasies are more complicated. When angry or disappointed with their adoptive parents, many conjure up images of idealized birth parents who are the perfect parents every child wishes for and who would give them everything they ever wanted. But for the fantasy to be effective for the adopted child, it must include some overriding and powerful explanation for the loss of the parents, that is, an explanation that in no way compromises their perfection. It must be entirely someone else's fault that the child is no longer with them.

An 8-year-old cultivated an elaborate fantasy that she could conjure up at will any time she felt angry at her adoptive parents. She called it "feeling orange at them." In this fantasy she had a mother who looked just like her and a father who looked like the prince in "Cinderella." They would come into her bedroom and hug her and hold her. They would always bring cookies and candy, read her stories, then take her for rides at the amusement park and on to McDonald's. They said that everything about her was good: she wasn't messy, she wasn't lazy, she wasn't rude. She was perfect and so were they—a far cry from the reality of her everyday life.

For many adopted children it is more difficult to develop this kind of reassuring fantasy since there is the complication of having to deal with already having "original" parents somewhere about whom they have fantasies. They are required to deal with disappointments and ambivalence toward two sets of parents. Fantasies of birth parents are based on the often-meager facts that have been shared with them. For example: "Your mother was too young, too poor, unmarried" or "Your parents couldn't raise another child." These facts conjure up disquieting images of inadequate, irresponsible, rejecting people. The explanation commonly offered that the birth mother loved the child so much she gave the child away so he or she could have a better life isn't very comforting to a child, to whom loving and giving away are not compatible.

Fantasies of adopted children involve trying to sort out responsibility and blame. For school-age children one logical conclusion is that if they were good, they would have been kept: "I must have been a bad baby and that's why she gave me away. I must have been too messy (like my room) or a crybaby (like someone called me yesterday) or a bad eater (like I was at lunch)." The fantasy may expand to include biological siblings who were or were not kept. One boy fantasized that he had a twin. He was the bad (throwaway) one while his twin brother was the good ("kept") child. He scanned shopping centers and movie theaters to get a glimpse of his ideal equivalent. Another logical conclusion is that the birth mother was a bad mother who gave away a good baby. "She was too busy going to parties to take care of me," said one boy. There may be moments of comfort in imagining a bad mother giving away all her good children or even a good mother giving away all her bad children. The notion of some children, or even one, being kept upsets the child's basic insistence on fairness.

The facts presented with the disclosure of the adoption are also critical to the child's identity formation. A child may wonder, "What does it mean about me that my parents were too young or too poor? Am I destined, then, to be just like them?"

Birthdays are a time when members of the adoption circle tend to be particularly aware of each other. Many adopted children begin to feel distressed in anticipation of the day. This distress is different from the usual excitement (and anxiety) biological children experience around their birthdays. Many adoptees think that if ever "she" would think of them it would certainly be this day. Some consciously and unconsciously await some sign—a card, a call, a visit—and find themselves disappointed when it doesn't occur. Each year, in a child's way of thinking, they must decide whose fault it is that the relinquishment occurred and assign "good and bad." The aftermath of a birthday can be a deflating, disappointing time, leaving the child with anger and lowered self-esteem and requiring a recovery period.

One youngster had an eventful fifth birthday party planned: his parents would take him and his best buddies to see the movie *Willy Wonka and the Chocolate Factory* and then to eat at the local pizza parlor, famous for children's birthday celebrations. But the movie had themes of bad, bratty children being flushed away like bad eggs. This usually resilient child became increasingly anxious as the film progressed; he climbed on his mother's lap and hid his eyes while his friends enjoyed the story with no noticeable distress. Tension continued after leaving the theater and peaked at the pizza parlor when he burst into tears as everyone sang "Happy Birthday" to him. Talking to his mother alone later, this verbally precocious child spoke of how terrified he was that the piano-playing lady at the local pizza parlor where he was having his birthday party was his birth mother and that she would take him away if she knew his identity. This terror reflected both a wish and a fear. He wished she would want him but was clearly bonded to his adoptive family and feared being taken away from them. The movie exacerbated already-existing "birthday worries" of being a bad, thrownaway baby, feelings that could be undone only if his birth mother decided he was good enough to retrieve.

At times, to protect themselves, children may need to blame

the adoptive parents. If children believe the birth parents were "bad," they, as their offspring, may feel imbued with this "badness." A way to defend against these feelings is to decide that they instead came from "good" stock and are thus "good" children. The "family romance" may become the belief that the birth parents were indeed nobility and that the child was kidnapped by the adoptive parents for their own selfish needs.

These wishes and fears, common to adopted children at this age, upset the sense of permanency of the adoptive relationship. Children may worry that if they were abandoned once, it might happen again. Some children have a need to test this out and may behave in ways that test their parents' patience and limits. Wondering what they did to deserve getting kicked out the first time, they experiment with what it would take to get kicked out again. In order to wage a real test, they will choose behaviors that they think were the ones that did them in the first time around or that they feel certain will provoke and offend parents now. One 8-year-old who had previously seemed well adjusted developed some odd "habits." He began not wiping himself clean after bowel movements so that his underwear was slightly soiled and smelly. He also began licking his lips frequently, causing unsightly irritation and scabs. He became a person who looked and smelled bad. It turned out that this was a reenactment of what he thought caused his original abandonment. When he was able to talk about this with his parents and receive their empathy and reassurances, he was able to give up these behaviors and move on.

The fact of adoption also stirs up the question of belonging. One youngster this age wondered what would happen to him if his adoptive parents died. Would he get returned to the adoption agency? Would he go to his birth parents? Being informed of guardianship arranged within the family comforted and reassured him. Through firmness and support from parents, the question of permanency may be answered and laid to rest for this time of life. It is likely to reemerge at later stages to be answered again.

As children enter the school system, their world enlarges. There is a wider community in which their adoption must be accepted as a fact of life. There may be some uncomfortable and even jarring moments when issues of heredity or lineage arise naturally in school programs. Children and adults may make insensitive or sometimes even cruel comments. One fourth-grade class was learning about different kinds of families. A very well liked girl described how she had been adopted as a baby. No one in the class would believe her. They insisted that she looked like her adoptive parents, that they were nice and she was nice and so she just couldn't be adopted. The children's images of adoptive families and their need to deny this uncomfortable fact about their classmate produced sheer disbelief. The girl came home from school quite shaken. She had been very comfortable in her family and comfortable with the reality of her adoption. Not long afterward a classmate informed her, "These are not your real parents. My mother told me your real parents gave you away." These reactions of her classmates suggested a stigma that she herself had not previously experienced and that now unnerved her.

School age is a phase of development in which, in Erikson's terms, children struggle with "industry versus inferiority."[4] It is a time when children seek recognition by producing things, by becoming workers, and begin taking pride in their adequacy. At the same time, they identify with their coworkers and join the ranks of adequate people. The issue of abandonment that adopted children confront during this phase tends to compromise their feelings of adequacy and call into question their basic human status. They fight feelings of being a castoff or of being inadequate, as they may perceive their birth parents to be. Even in the best of circumstances—a sturdy, bright, healthy, attractive child with understanding, loving adoptive parents—this struggle for a sense of an adequate self is a mighty battle. Anything less than "good enough" circumstances, such as a physical or mental anomaly or intolerance and rejection on the part of adoptive parents, contributes further to a sense of inferiority and poor functioning.

Struggling with these issues, however difficult, is a normal and necessary process for adopted children and is reflected in their fantasies. However, fantasies, such as those described in the previous paragraphs are part of the child's own private world. Some children are more expressive than others about their private thoughts and feelings. They sometimes invite parents' inclusion through words and sometimes through behavior. The 5-year-old who experienced troublesome birth parent fantasies at his birthday party first exhibited his distress through his behavior and then talked with his mother, who had expressed concern about him. It was necessary for this mother to provide an atmosphere that communicated to her son that his feelings were respected, that they were speakable, and that no harm would come to their relationship if he expressed them. In this atmosphere he could unburden himself and receive comfort and support. Not all children are as verbal as this boy. All parents need to work toward a balance of respect for their child's privacy and sensitivity to their ongoing struggles. It is a delicate lifelong dance.

PHASE 6: PUBERTY AND ADOLESCENCE

In western society, adolescence is universally considered a major developmental stage. Relevant tasks are commonly thought to be the gradual formation of an individual identity that allows for a genuine separateness as well as an emotional tie to one's family. Achieving this kind of balance tends to be difficult. In the course of the process, adolescents often feel the task is impossible: How can you be your own person, they wonder, and also remain acceptable enough to your parents to maintain a civilized relationship with them? How can you be committed to your peer group at the same time you are committed to your family? While many adults may wish they had managed their own adolescent years differently, few would like to go back and reexperience those years. Most parents of adolescents find this a very troublesome stage. They complain about their teenagers' tumultuous shifts from dependency to independence and back again, as well as the shifts from being like them to being sometimes outrageously unlike them. "One day, there is not a thing I can cook that will suit her; the next day she won't leave the kitchen, licking the bowl of everything I prepare," lamented one mother. This process of struggling with separateness, experimenting with shifting identities and moving in and out of the family, is a common and sometimes rocky road for both adolescents and their parents.

Adoption issues are highly resonant to adolescent issues, and they interact in a way that exacerbates and sometimes inflames normal adolescent developmental tasks. For adoptees, it is not enough to integrate internal stirrings with the known external environment. Achieving the nonadoptee's tasks of developing a separate identity within and establishing appropriate independence from the family is only one piece of the charge for the adoptee. There is an entire other world—of the birth parents and fantasies of them—to process as these adolescents attempt to determine what kind of adult they can or will become.

Many will insist that these phantoms are not relevant. Mark, a 14-year-old, became very irritated with his therapist when she (once again) suggested that his disruptive behavior was related to feelings about being abandoned by his birth mother. He exploded, shouting, "My birth mother, my birth mother—that's all you ever talk about. And I don't even think about her half the time!" Even "half the time" is an indication of the profound presence of these figures.

From the earliest moments of puberty adoptees wonder who they are and who they are like as developing adults. They scan the environment to find some anchoring points with which to identify. As the beginning signs of bodily changes are observed, the adoptee imagines the end results and what they mean. There is no visible biological parent with whom to compare. Girls want to know how big their mother's breasts became, when their mothers reached menarche, and how bad her cramps were. Boys want to know about their father's physiques and how they developed. Knowing that your mother was "petite" or that your father was "heavyset" is not much to go on when you are trying to figure out who you are likely to become.

What the pubescent adoptees do know about their birth parents is that they were sexually active and usually irresponsible about birth control. Observing the development of their own characteristics can be a distressing and complicating factor, evoking both the wish and the fear of being like the birth parents. Susan, a 13-year-old who had enjoyed a warm and easygoing relationship with her parents, become very irritable and moody in the early stages of breast development. She had also become extremely modest about nudity and militant about her privacy. Her parents chalked this behavior up to puberty and optimistically prepared themselves to ride it out. However, it seemed more excessive than that of other 13-year-olds they knew. One day when her mother accidentally walked in on her while she was dressing and was bare-chested, Susan flew into a rage, screaming, crying, and hurling valued objects around her room. She ended up sobbing in her mother's arms and expressing her desperation about her developing breasts. She was terrified at her emerging sexuality, fearing that she would turn out to be a "slut," as she thought her birth mother had been. Her mother's emotional availability and reassurance were comforting and reduced the crisis for the time being. Later, in therapy, it became apparent that some piece of Susan's fear was also a wish. She saw her adoptive mother as too plain and unsexy. There was a part of her that wanted to be more like her image of her birth mother. In time, Susan was able to reconcile both parts of herself and achieve an identity separate from both her birth mother and her adoptive mother.

A 14-year-old boy became similarly distressed when he found himself having wet dreams. He concluded that the lustfulness behind his wet dreams meant that he was an uncontrolled "stud," as he imagined his birth father to be. Sometimes he thought this was "cool," but at other times he believed it was "gross" and irresponsible. Sexual identification thus becomes complicated as adoptees attempt to integrate their inner impulses with their identification with their adoptive parents and with the facts, as well as their fantasies, about their birth parents. Depending on their current needs, adoptees may accept or reject identification with birth parents and adoptive parents. They may identify themselves, intermittently or consistently, as asexual or overly responsible to be sure they will not turn out like their birth parents. Sorting out these identifications requires dealing with wishes and fears, as well as feelings of loyalty and disloyalty to both sets of parents.

Adoptees' sexual identifications with birth parents are sometimes a way of protecting those parents and at the same time protecting themselves. Behaving as they imagined their birth parents behaved is a way of saying, "My roots weren't so bad; I'm just like her (or him)." While there are no conclusive statistics to substantiate the belief, most child welfare workers' experience is that adopted adolescents tend to act out sexually more than nonadopted adolescents, placing adopted girls at greater risk for pregnancy.

Some adopted girls seem compelled to repeat their birth mother's experience, perhaps unconsciously feeling this is the only way they can really understand what happened. Having failed to cognitively understand how a mother could give a child away, they attempt to understand it experientially. They frequently place themselves in an untenable situation, that is, without internal or external resources to care for a child—the same circumstance in which they imagine their mothers to have been in. The occurrence of the pregnancy often seems "out of character" for the girl; that is, it happens to girls who seem otherwise well adjusted, in control of themselves, and seemingly responsible about sexuality and birth control. Despite this high functioning, the question of how it came about that they were relinquished remains such a powerful one that adopted girls may be driven to uncharacteristic behavior in an effort to find an answer.

Another possible conscious or unconscious motivation of an adopted girl who becomes pregnant is to do something her adoptive mother was unable to do. This may be based on competitive feelings and may be a way of surpassing a mother an adoptee may have felt she could not measure up to. Or the pregnancy may, instead, be based on a need to fulfill the adoptive couple's long-term unmet wish—to have a baby born in the household. In some ways, the girl's pregnancy may be the ultimate gift to the adoptive parents, one that can be neither perceived nor appreciated since the circumstances surrounding it are so distressing. One 15-year-old adoptee produced such a "gift." In this family the adoptive parents care for the baby virtually full-time while the girl lives with her 18-year-old husband in the basement apartment. Recently, the 15-year-old's mother announced that she was going with the baby to visit her own mother in California so the infant could meet "her grandmother" when in fact *she* was the grandmother.

The outcome of the pregnancy of an adopted girl is likely to be determined on the basis of the girl's fantasies about her birth mother's experience and her adoptive mother's experience and what they mean to her. The young woman may want to keep the child to do what she thinks her mother wanted to do or should have done, thus undoing the "mistake." For example, a girl who has convinced herself that her mother was forced to give her up may undo that event by insisting, "No one will force me to give away my baby—no matter what!" She, in one act, takes care of herself and her birth mother.

Or the adolescent may place her child for adoption in order to affirm, perhaps even forgive, her birth mother's decision. She may feel that she can now understand the necessity of her mother's relinquishment of her. She perceives relinquishment as a required act for her own survival and for the best interests of her child. In deciding it is acceptable for herself, she also decides it was acceptable for her birth mother. However, if she has perceived her adoptive mother's wish for a baby, relinquishment may also represent a hostile act toward her.

Aborting the pregnancy may be an adolescent adoptee's way of aborting herself and destroying the child who should never have been conceived. On the other hand, an abortion may be her way of indicating genuine differentiation from her birth mother by exercising an alternative that is best for her.

Adopted boys may also be compelled to somehow repeat the

unplanned pregnancy drama. They may become irresponsible, as they imagined their birth fathers to have been, or superresponsible to make up for the past. They may pressure their lover to abort, keep, or place the child, depending on where their own identification and needs lie. Adolescent adoptees need their parents' help in recognizing that their sexuality is a normal developing part of themselves and not evidence of a predetermined life path.

In addition to sexual identification, a more general ego identity formation is taking place. The adoptee asks, "Who am I and whom am I like?" Adoptive parents provide one set of possible identifications, in social class, lifestyle, career choices, and so forth. But adoptees also have facts and fantasies of birth parents to integrate. Most commonly, they have been given bits of information to go on: "Your mother was musically talented"; "Your father was athletic"; "Your parents were unskilled workers"; "Your mother dropped out of school in the 11th grade"; "Your parents were college students." The commonality here is that all the birth parents found they were unwilling or unable to keep and raise the child they had borne. For the adoptee this may mean that in addition to being irresponsible about birth control, the birth parents were "inadequate" people, unable to provide for their own offspring, or "selfish," unwilling to put their own needs aside for the sake of their child. An adoptee may ask, "Does this mean I come from bad stock?" or "Am I destined to also function poorly?" Although adolescent adoptees may believe that relinquishment is a perfectly good decision and one they would emulate, it is difficult for them to accept the decision on an emotional level. Thus, the facts about and personality descriptions of their birth parents may produce powerfully ambivalent feelings about the similarities or dissimilarities between them.

One young teenager, Margaret, had been told that her birth mother was very artistic. Her adoptive father was also artistic. While the girl herself had artistic ability, her parents observed that she seemed resistant to develop this skill. Feeling overwhelmed by what felt like a "choice" between being like an inadequate woman or an adequate man, Margaret fled the conflict by simply avoiding that part of her personality. In so doing, she denied herself (and her family) the pleasures of her talent.

Mark, a bright, handsome, and talented 14-year-old, was notably unsuccessful in all areas of his life. Having been told that his birth parents had been unable to take care of him, he imagined them to be totally nonfunctioning street people. In therapy it became apparent that Mark unconsciously felt that if he became too successful or too prominent, his birth parents would discover who he was and come to him to be salvaged. He cited the example of a local self-made man who had become the object of innumerable philanthropic requests. To avoid this stress and responsibility, Mark maintained a low profile of mediocrity. As he came to understand this about himself, he became increasingly able to function to his own potential.

The struggle with integrating parental identity figures does not always involve such negative interferences as in the cases of Mark and Margaret. Some adoptees may experience getting the best of both worlds. When the worlds are very different, it takes some effort to put them together. Jimmy, 16, was a strapping athlete, most unlike his slight, short, adoptive father. The family culture tended to be intellectual and artistic and few members had much good physical coordination or interest in sports, an environment that might seem like a "poor match" for Jimmy. Instead, the differences between the biology of the child and the psychology of the family became a circumstance that enriched the lives of all. Jimmy brought something new to the family that they were able to appreciate and enjoy. He felt valued for his physical qualities. At the same time, the intelligence and sensitivity in the family contributed to Jimmy's development and allowed him to become far more than a "jock." "We opened up new worlds to each other and we are all better off for it," Jimmy's mother concluded. In all these areas of identity formation, the tasks for adoptees are to confront and recognize the biological and psychological parts of themselves as real, to deny neither one nor the other, and to give neither undue weight. This recognition is the beginning of developing an integrated, cohesive sense of oneself.

Adolescence is a stage of development marked by strivings for independence and separation. Many teenagers wouldn't be caught dead being seen with their parents at a shopping mall and take great pride in their separate peer life. Often through trial and error, they learn what they can, in fact, do on their own and what help they continue to need from their parents. With experience and increasing competence, they move toward a launching into the adult world.

For adoptees, separation and independence have some special meanings. They have been abandoned by their birth parents and have lost the inviolable biological tie. For them, separation may imply a second abandonment. They may fear that the loss of the adoptive parents' childrearing function may mean the end of the relationship, that it may be, in effect, an eviction rather than a launching. They may feel terrified at the thought of being out in the world alone, without an anchoring point, and may need to test again the strength of the tie.

One way of dealing with feelings of a second abandonment is to turn the passive, helpless feelings into active, powerful ones. Instead of risking being left again, adoptees may take it upon themselves to do the leaving. They may do it in a dramatic manner by running away or in a more subdued fashion by becoming aloof and elusive, thus placing parents in the position of constantly taking the initiative in the relationship (in a way, these adolescents keep their parents searching for them). Out of this fear of abandonment, adolescents may fantasize finding their birth parents so that they can reattach and undo both the original abandonment and what they feel is an impending one.

Late adolescence is a time when adoptees may, for many reasons, begin expressing interest in their biological families to learn more about them and about themselves. They struggle with this information in regard to their identity formation and also in regard to separation. The easiest way to separate from someone you feel very attached to is to decide you do not like them anymore. Adolescents are notorious for their criticisms of their parents, who do not seem to know how to do anything right anymore. They sometimes pit them against other parents who are viewed as much superior.

This increased interest in birth parents, the faultfinding, and the distancing may be very difficult for adoptive parents, who may feel they are losing their child rather than experiencing a normal though complicated developmental stage. Long-term fears of birth parents retrieving the child may be heightened as the child goes through the permutations of separation. Some parents may feel so rejected and hurt that they reject in return: ''If he doesn't want us, we don't want him.'' Thus, they fulfill the adolescent's prophecy. Other parents may find themselves trying to hold on tighter, thus causing the child to pull away even harder.

The adolescent adoptee's separation and search for independence can be a kind of recapitulation of the original homecoming and early bonding process. Adoptees and their parents again look each other over, feel each other out, acknowledge the existence of the birth parents, and reexplore what kind of a tie they will have with each other. These pushes and pulls during the adolescent years are a part of the process of accepting a different model of a family. Adoptive parents and adolescents alike must accept the family's different parts so that the child can move further toward achieving a feeling of independence rather than of eviction. When this begins to occur, parent and child can begin a kind of recontracting in which they agree that their relationship is a permanent one based on their life experience together rather than on blood ties and that this permanence transcends whatever relationship the child chooses to develop directly or symbolically with his birth parents. This contract cannot truly be completed until there is an integration of the biological and psychological parts of identity and a consolidation of the efforts toward separation and independence, achievements that cannot be expected until the adult years.

Life events such as illness, death, or divorce of adoptive parents have special significance for adoptees. They already carry with them a vulnerability in terms of their legitimacy, their losses, and their concerns about being bad and causing trouble. How they respond to life events will depend on their personality structure, the status of their existing relationships, and their developmental stage. Some adoptees will navigate these difficult events quite adequately. Those who are struggling with vulnerabilities that are particularly touched by these events may be overwhelmed. For example, four-year-olds, still in the mode of magical thinking, will conclude that their adopted mother's death was a result of their own angry thoughts. They will believe this was the *second* mother they have destroyed. A 13-year-old boy who is at a sensitive developmental age for issues of separation may have a very difficult time with his adoptive parents' divorce. His developmental need is to make early moves away from his parents; instead, his parents' divorce removes the structure he needs to push up against. In addition, he has added proof that families do not stay together. He may wonder, again, if he is really wanted by any parent as his adoptive parents go on to their new, separate lives. His parents' continuing commitment and support over time may provide sufficient support for the boy to resume his developmental course. Remarriages of adoptive parents will present all the usual challenges of blended families. Stepparents will need to be distinguished from adoptive parents, and if either parent produces a biological child with the new partner, issues of feeling like the second choice or second best may reemerge. Again, the security of the preexisting parent–child relationship will be crucial to the adoptee's ability to weather this life transition.

PHASE 7: YOUNG ADULTHOOD

Young adults are in an unattached state—between their family of origin and the life they choose for their adult years. This transition involves choices of work life and intimate relationships. There is a process of deciding which aspects of the life of the family of origin to maintain, which to modify, and which to leave behind. It is a continuation of the adolescent process of separation with further refinement of the definitions of identity and connectedness to family. The choices made regarding new relationships and work life are statements about the maturational progress of this developing adult.

For adoptees, this state of transition and the choices of work and intimacy are more complicated. They have two families of origin rather than one and, thus, many more factors to consider in deciding what to keep, modify, or discard. The tie to family involves both an attachment to the adoptive family and a concern about genealogical continuity. These are expressed in the following questions reported by one young man:

> "Who am I? What do I present to the world out there as I explore intimate relationships and work? Am I really a college graduate prepared for a professional life like my adoptive parents or have I just been groomed to look like one? Sometimes I feel like a total fraud and that I am really an auto mechanic dressed up to look like a lawyer. In fact, I don't feel comfortable as either. It makes me confused, too, about what kind of a woman I want to marry. I want someone who would be as comfortable with an auto mechanic as she would be with a college professor. I know that is unrealistic but, in fact, that's how I feel. I am very confused and lost. I just don't know what I want."

So the question of "Who am I?" continues to be salient in the choice of work and love. One young woman who had been told that her birth mother had dropped out of school observed that many girls she knew who dropped out of school went to beauty school. She was determined to become a hairdresser despite her lack of aptitude with hair and her exceptional abilities in other areas. The least conflictual process occurs when the reported facts or the fantasies regarding birth parents seem to also apply to the adoptive family. Stacey had been told that her birth parents were bright college kids who loved each other but were not ready to marry and raise a child. She imagined that they both, very much like her adoptive parents, went on to successful professional careers, and she had no difficulty doing this herself. She later married her college sweetheart. Adoptees continue to attempt to sort out genealogy in attempting to establish themselves in the adult world and in a lifestyle that works and feels comfortable.

One real fear (conscious or unconscious) of adoptees is that they will inadvertently marry a biological relative. Occasionally, there is a newspaper report of a couple who are lovers or who marry and then find out that they are biological siblings. Tabloid sheets sometimes headline such revealed incestuous relationships. One young man reported spending hours trying to figure out a foolproof method of selecting a mate guaranteed not to be related to him. Being biracial, he could not rule out all black or all white women or any age groups since his birth parents were not married to each other and could have reproduced at any time. He thus had ruled out everybody and was a very lonely fellow.

A girl in her early twenties spoke of an intense relationship she had in college. In her growing-up days she had an active fantasy of having a biological brother who looked very much like her. She was constantly on the lookout for him. In college she came upon just such a young man. In fact, they looked so much alike that classmates teased them about being twins. She felt very distressed at her attraction toward him and found herself alternately getting close to and then distancing herself from him. No amount of surreptitiously gathered family history from him sufficiently reassured her. She finally ended the relationship, breaking both their hearts.

Some adoptees "never even think about it half the time" but find themselves discarding one potential mate after another and never being quite sure why. Others may establish a set of exclusion criteria for a safe choice. They may decide, for example, that they would be safe with all Caucasian, all black, or all Hispanic mates and find themselves attracted only to the acceptable group. "I don't know, I just like them better" would be their subjective experience. Parents may be dismayed at this propensity. Their efforts to expand their children's choices may be met with a rigid resistance reflective of what the young adults feel is an investment in their own survival and genealogy. Given all these complications, it is likely that adoptees will need additional time to choose a mate.

As we have already seen, being "unattached" has different implications for adopted young adults. They must learn through everyday experience that leaving home means neither abandonment nor eviction. They must see that the adoptive family remains an anchoring point of departure. Even if the separation was a rocky one—including the extreme of placement outside the home—the bonds can remain constant and the emotional tie unbreakable. Some adoptees (and parents) may need to "cut off" for a time to test this bond; in a few cases the mutual need for cutoff between parent and child may prove irreparable.

These disquieting issues motivate many young adults to search for their birth parents for some answers. Some seek information only and have no stated wish to have personal contact. Some want information, reunion, and continuing relationships with birth parents. In addition to the difference in goals, there are differences in the intensity with which adoptees pursue these goals. For some there is a feeling of urgency and a sense that they cannot be complete people without a confrontation with the genetic parts of themselves. Others feel less urgent but eager for such information to enrich their sense of well-being.

A recent study describes the experience of 114 adoptees who had reunions with their birth parents.[5] Of these, 101 actively searched and 13 were found. Most of the searchers (103) were women and 62% were affiliated with an adoption reform group. The vast majority were adopted through agencies before they were six months old. Contrary to previous studies the results here indicated that searchers were not unhappy with their adoptive families.[6,7] They decided to search out of four basic motivations: a life cycle transition (as with the birth of a first child), desire for information, hope for a relationship with the birth parent, and wish for self-understanding. The outcome was overwhelmingly reported as successful, with only two people feeling any negative effects. This study made no mention of the "genetic erotic attraction" described by birth mothers (see note 15, Chapter 2, and the discussion in that chapter). This is most likely due to the design of the questionnaire but may also be attributed to adoptees' reluctance to discuss such feelings. The authors note the highly selective quality of their sample and caution against generalizing the results to the whole population of adult adoptees. They comment that "adoptees who search seem to be looking for ways to build an extended nuclear family, not to replace their adopted family. They seem to need to bring the two parts of themselves together so that they can build a sense of self that feels complete to them."[8] The authors suggest that adoptive parents be prepared for this need in their children.

Other adoptees reject the idea of a search. There are those who feel angry and rejected: "If they haven't wanted to look for me, I sure as hell don't want to look for them." There are others who feel very satisfied and comfortable with their lives and don't feel there is a great deal to be gained from such a search. One such 20- year-old said, "I prefer the magic of the mystery." Others fear that a reunion may bring on problems for them in having to attend to the needs of an additional set of parents.

We are increasingly seeing the formation of adoptee support groups as men and women seek support and understanding of these struggles. However, because the issues also emerge in family discussions, in friendships, and in therapy, it is important to recognize the normalcy of the questions and of the discomfort. The difficult process of integrating one's identity and coming to terms with the lack of genealogical continuity is likely to prolong the ordinary tasks of young adulthood. It is more difficult to decide what kind of work to choose when there are models based on both fantasy and reality. It is more difficult to choose a mate when the family includes actual members as well as phantoms. Since the process of "ruling out" and "ruling in" has so many factors, it may take longer to come to comfortable conclusions. The adoptee may seem to be floundering. Parents can be supportive by understanding how complicated and conflictual this period may be and by recognizing that this process may take longer than it did with their friends' biological children. As this integration of identity occurs, there is a recontracting with the adoptive family and, sometimes, the establishment of a relationship with the birth parents' family, to include all members of the circle.

PHASE 8: ADULTHOOD

As adoptees move on into adulthood, a shifting of generation and generational roles occurs. They become heads of their own new households while their parents move on to become the elders. Caretaking roles begin to be more mutual. Adults may begin to look after their parents by inviting them to their homes and providing hospitality. They become more, if not completely, financially self-sufficient, and the elders begin focusing more on how they will take care of themselves in their later years.

A complication in making this shift for adoptees is the sense that society continues to see them as "adopted children," no matter how old they become. Sorosky, Baran, and Pannor, in *The Adoption Triangle*, refer to this as the "perennial child role" and give an example of a 40-year-old woman who needed her 67-year-old mother's permission to seek information from the agency that had arranged for her adoption.[9] The authors suggest that the role is "perpetuated by the possessiveness and overprotectiveness of the adoptive parents." Again, we see circumstances that may prolong the completion of developmental tasks.

For adoptees, the birth of a child has special meaning. They achieve the reality of having a blood relative in their lives, perhaps for the very first time. The baby may be the first flesh-and-blood relation the adoptee is able to see and touch. Even when the experiences in the adoptive family have been excellent, procreation can be a poignant and highly significant event. "As much as I loved my Mom and Dad, it was especially wonderful to look at someone who looked like me. I had always wished for that with them. In fact, I used to want to dye my hair to match my mother's," said one woman. A new father was surprised at how touched he felt when his baby boy had his funny ears. He reported feeling overwhelmingly attached to him in a way he had never felt before. "I didn't know what I was missing," he mused.

Adoptive parents who have worked through their own reproductive issues and have come to genuinely accept the differences of the adoptive family will be happy for their children to have this heartwarming experience. Those who have not may find it threatening, experiencing envy and fearing once again that they may lose their child to a blood relative.

Having, keeping, and raising a child of one's own is likely to stir up old and new feelings about birth parents. Even during the pregnancy, there may be concerns about what heredity is likely to produce. While most biological parents report concerns about having a "normal" baby or fear some known inheritable condition, adoptees must deal with a fear of the unknown. Was there some racial mixture that could emerge in this generation? Were there any unreported diseases or conditions that might affect my baby? Some adoptees report overwhelming anxiety about being able to produce a normal child. Spouses and relatives may feel and express similar concerns, all of which may contribute to the urge to search. At the same time, there may be a benevolent wish to let birth parents know that they have become grandparents and to mark the significance of this milestone. There may be a need to address the relinquishment at a time when it may feel inconceivable to give up a child. Or it may now seem very understandable how a person who was too young, single, or poor would opt out of the formidable task of childrearing, and some adoptees may want to express their forgiveness. Adoptees may also feel empathy for their birth parents' loss. Susan R experienced severe anxiety several months after her daughter was born. In therapy she expressed the fear that she would lose what she valued most—her husband and her baby. What emerged from her therapeutic work was a sense of guilt that she was enjoying a life of which she imagined her birth mother had been deprived. With this understanding, her anxiety diminished.

With the adoptee's independence and reproduction comes a further shift of roles: children become parents; parents become grandparents. Different kinds of caregiving begin to occur, with the middle generation beginning to watch over the children and the parents.

At some point there is the task of disclosing one's adoption to one's own children. In doing so, there is likely to be a resurgence of the anguish originally experienced in feeling atypical or imperfect in some way. At the same time, adoptees may reach a new understanding of the adoptive parents' anguish as they find how hard it is to tell their own children that they have grandparents they might never know or to respond to their child's horror in hearing that a parent could give a child away. In addition to an awareness of the special tasks required of them as adoptees, there may now be a new awareness of the special tasks that adoptive parents have struggled with for so many years.

With mastery of these tasks of adulthood, adoptees greet the new generation with an increased sense of integration of their biological and psychological pasts, both of which contribute to the development of the next generation.

PHASE 9: LATER LIFE

Developmental tasks of later life include dealing with changing life circumstances. There may be loss of parents, declining health, death or divorce of a spouse, grandparenthood, job retirement, or financial strain. Once again, for the adoptee these changing circumstances carry with them some added burdens and complications.

The loss of an adoptive parent involves the genuine loss of the real relationship, whatever that may have been. At the same time, the loss may relieve the adoptee of some burden of loyalty and feelings of protection toward the parent with respect to his or her longings for the birth parents. Studies of searchers indicate that many adoptees postpone a research until adoptive parents—and particularly adoptive mothers—have died. The expressed feeling around this decision is a wish not to hurt the adoptive parent, out of respect and gratitude for their care. There may also be a fear of anger or retribution, and some may be seeking a "back-up" mother to replace the one lost. Also related to the timing of a search at this time may be a feeling that it is "now or never" in regard to the aging birth parents. Indeed, there may be some wish to tend to an aging parent who may be needful, as was done—or not done—for the adoptive parent.

Death or divorce of a spouse may be especially difficult for an adoptee since it may trigger his or her most profound vulnerability—the feeling of abandonment. Particularly if such an event is accompanied by declining health or financial stress, there may be a revisiting of the "abandoned orphan" feelings previously experienced.

OUTCOME FOR ADOPTEES

The earliest and most frequently reported findings in the adoption literature were those that clinicians in inpatient, outpatient, and residential treatment settings provided. All these settings reported an overrepresentation of adopted children in their populations. Such children made up from 4% to 15% of the clinical population, although they constituted only 2% of the population at large. They were particularly overrepresented in the inpatient and residential treatment centers, a fact that is suggestive of more serious dysfunction.

This overrepresentation is so consistently reported and frequently replicated over the years across settings as to be an accepted fact. Why there is such an overrepresentation is still unclear. It is possible that the facts speak for themselves and that adopted children (for whatever reasons) have more emotional and behavioral problems and thus are aptly overrepresented in mental health facilities. But other explanations are also possible.

One is that adoptive parents tend to be representative of a more educated, higher socioeconomic class whose members would be more likely to turn to mental health professionals and therefore their children are no more overrepresented than are the biological children of demographically similar parents. Another possibility is that adoptive parents, having successfully turned to agencies to receive their child, feel more trusting and more ready to seek further help than their nonadoptive counterparts. Some clinicians have suggested other psychological motivations for adoptive parents, for instance, a secret wish to return the child to an agency or to have the agency "fix" what they feel are damaged goods.

Research suggests some differences in presenting symptomatology between adopted children and nonadoptees. Adoptees are more likely to present with problems of an acting-out nature, such as lying, stealing, running away, impulsivity, and aggression, as well as with learning difficulties and attention deficit disorders. Many explanations of these difficulties are offered. Psychoanalysts were the first to begin to identify problems of adoptees as they presented themselves in psychotherapy. These reports were based almost entirely on children and adolescents; there were almost no reports on adult adoptees (it may have been that adoptive status was generally overlooked as a significant factor in the emotional life of adult patients).

Paul Brinich, one of the early psychoanalytic writers on adoption, noted common themes that emerge in the treatment of adoptees.[10] One theme is a sense of being unwanted, rejected, or abandoned by birth parents. They then struggle with why they were unwanted and whose fault it was—their own or their birth parents'. Adoptive parents are sometimes pitted against birth parents to determine who is "good" or "bad." During adolescence adoptees attempt to separate from both adoptive parents and images of birth parents in determining their sense of self and identity.[11] This struggle can be more or less intense, with some adoptees identifying with adoptive parents and also identifying with their fantasized images of birth parents. Others may feel less of a struggle and more easily integrate their biological heritage with their adoptive upbringing. Out of these clinical experiences with referred adoptees, clinicians conclude that these children are susceptible to a greater psychological risk than are nonadoptees. These writers also describe the kinds of psychological issues adoptive parents confront and the possible effects of these issues on the children. Clinicians cite adoptive parents' unresolved conflicts regarding infertility, the idealized fantasies of their biological child, and marital problems as significant factors in the development of the adopted child.[12,13,14]

There are few studies comparing adoptees and nonadoptees in a non-clinical population. Those that do exist indicate a more mixed picture of adjustment. Studies of elementary school–age children have focused primarily on personality development and school and social adjustment. Some studies found little significant differences between the two groups on these characteristics[15] while others found some significant differences, particularly in school-related behavior.[16,17,18] Despite these differences, adoptees' adjustments were still found to be within normal limits. In the more recent studies adopted children were seen to have more symptomatology and their behavior fell within a maladaptive range.[19] The authors of this study consider the possibility that the middle childhood years and the need to adjust to the school environment are particularly stressful for children struggling to understand what it means to be adopted.

The few studies done comparing adopted and nonadopted adolescents also yielded mixed findings. One study measuring self-concept found adoptees scoring more positively than their counterparts,[20] while a study of identity formation using a variety of scales found them to have lower self-esteem, poorer socialization skills, and higher impulsivity.[21] The most extensive study on adolescents done so far is the longitudinal Delaware Family Study, which found no significant differences in identity formation issues.[22]

Each of these studies raises important questions as we try to assess how adopted children fare along their developmental paths. Unfortunately, research to date has been so flawed methodologically that it offers us few answers. The limitations derive from being based on few clinical cases, on anecdotal reports, on a highly selected sample of volunteers or support group members, and on an extremely small sample size. We are hearing about a very small percentage of adoptees who become known to researchers either by becoming a part of the clinical population or by volunteering through preselected support groups. We know little about the masses of adoptees who do not make their presence known in these ways. More importantly, there has been no significant research on adoptees once they research adulthood. They are rarely mentioned in psychological literature and have not been noted to be overrepresented in mental health facilities, as they were as children.

Researchers' efforts to assess how adoptees fare have thus focused on adjustment problems during childhood and adolescence. When comparisons are made, control groups are nonadoptees. To accurately assess the welfare of adoptees, their functioning would also need to be compared with children who experienced the actual alternative—being raised by unprepared birth parents.

CONCLUSION

By tracing the developmental tasks of adoptees, it is clear that they face special issues and challenges. They have to confront the fact of their relinquishment and then make sense of it in the context of their adoptive family experience. The relinquishment represents a physical loss and the emotional loss of normal status. It naturally raises questions about the implications of this event for themselves.

All adoptees struggle with the significance of the fact of their relinquishment. Given differing personalities, some will "think it out," some will "talk it out," some will "act it out," and some will resort to a combination of these approaches. Adoptive parents provide the most positive context for this resolution when they are clearly committed to the permanency of the relationship and can accept their child's special tasks.

It may sometimes be unclear whether an adoptee is struggling adequately with those special tasks or whether he or she, in fact, needs some extra help. How does a parent or adoptee know when it is necessary to seek such help? Two guidelines may be useful. The first is that adoptees need help when they are fixed in their development and seem unable to progress. For example, if they are unable to test the permanency of their relationship with their adoptive parents and then move on, and instead remain mired in a provocative struggle with them, they need help with whatever is keeping them stuck. Or if, in processing the news of their adoption, they cannot get beyond blaming their adoptive parents for their relinquishment, they need someone besides their parents to talk to.

A second guideline is that adoptees need help when they detour significantly from their own developmental track, that is, when they "opt out" instead of attempting mastery, which naturally includes digressions and regressions. This opting out may take many forms, including dysfunctional behavior and consistent disturbances of mood.

Even in the very best of family circumstances, the inherent nature of adoptees' issues may make it more difficult for them to discuss their internal conflicts with their adoptive parents. The neutrality of a support group or a therapist is thus sometimes necessary and can be highly effective in helping adoptees get unstuck and back on a healthy developmental course.

Whether they needed therapy or not, adoptees are likely (and accurately) to feel that they went through more and "sweated" more than nonadopted people. Hopefully, in whatever way is right for them, they sort out the "facts" of their lives, lives that along the way felt so incongruous and so conflictual. Through this process, they can come to accept that adoption is not a matter of good and bad adults or good and bad children. It is, instead, a matter of life circumstances. Mastery requires a genuine acceptance of those life circumstances and the paradoxes they create. Satisfaction can be taken in this mastery, with full respect given to the wish that it could have been different.

CHAPTER 5

SHARED LIVES

*Interrelationship of Developmental Tasks
of Birth Parents, Adoptive Parents
and Adoptees*

THE ADOPTION CIRCLE IS FORMED to meet significant needs of each of its members and thus serve the greatest social good. In previous chapters we have seen how birth parents, adoptive parents, and adoptees travel their developmental courses and work toward mastery of their special tasks. By so doing, they maximize the positive qualities of adoption, a solution to the alternatives of raising a child before being ready to do so, being raised by an unready parent, or remaining childless.

As we have seen by tracing the developmental tasks of each member of the adoption circle, all members continue to be variously present in each other's lives over the course of the entire life span. This presence involves both fantasy and reality. In reality, adoptive parents and their children have daily contact with each other and, with more recent openness in adoption, may have some kind of indirect or direct contact with birth parents. In confidential adoptions we have seen evidence of the rich and intense fantasies that each member has about the absent participant—the ghosts that are "present but not present " every day. Adoptees fantasize about birth parents. They fantasize about who they are, where they are, how they look, what kind of family and work life they have, why they gave them up. Birth parents have similar fantasies about their relinquished children. They, too, imagine what they may look like with each passing year, how they are adjusting to home and school, and what ideas and feelings their child may have about the relinquishment. Birth parents and adoptive parents also fantasize about each other. They develop images of each other's functioning and the implications of that functioning for their mutual child. Each wonders and worries about what the other may be thinking about him or her.

As members proceed along their own developmental course, there are times when individual issues interrelate and have impact on one another. This impact can be positive and supportive of the adaptive qualities of the circle, with each member appreciating its advantages over its real alternatives. It can, also contribute to a dysfunction, miring the circle in a "stuckness" from which it is difficult for members to emerge. There are variations in these dynamics over time as individuals and the system proceed along the lifelong developmental course.

While each member has his or her own unique place and experience in the circle, there are some major themes that members have in common. The first is that all members of the circle deal with loss, and sometimes with related anger. No member willfully chooses the deprivation he or she experiences. Each feels like a helpless participant and thus must deal with the natural anger related to such feelings of helplessness. Adoption circle members may have difficulty modulating the resulting aggression toward themselves and others.

The second common theme is that all members deal with ordinary issues of attachment and separation in a way that is complicated by their knowledge of their genealogical discontinuity. The blood tie that links biological families is missing in the adoption circle, making attachments and separations less secure and fraught with anxiety that requires attention and resolution.

The third theme has to do with identity formation. Being adopted, adopting a child or relinquishing a child are experiences that cause adoption circle members to struggle with concerns about their authenticity: "Who am I and what does it mean about me that I am a part of this unusual arrangement? Am I really who I seem to be? Am I all right?"

Members of each segment of the circle have their own paradoxical components: adoptees are their birth parents' biological children but not their children by rearing, their adoptive parents' children by rearing but not by birth; birth parents are biological parents but not rearing parents; adoptive parents are rearing parents but not biological parents. There are times when, in fantasy and in reality, members support each other in what they are rather than what they are not. At other times there is a stronger focus on what is missing. Let us look now at these interrelationships and their impact.

FAMILY ORGANIZATION

Individuals in families organize into a system. Each system has a power structure, roles and functions, values and goals, and ways of communicating words and feelings. As family members travel the life cycle, there are necessary shifts in these components of the system to allow for individual growth. In good enough circumstances the system provides a point of attachment while allowing for appropriate individual strivings. The family is thus balanced through a flexibility that protects the group and also values and responds to individuals' needs.

The adoptive family system is complicated by the phenomenon that images of significant members are developed primarily through fantasy or what we might call mythology. This mythology, in turn, contributes to the family organization.

Antonio Ferreira describes a family myth as

a series of fairly well integrated beliefs shared by all family members concerning each other and their mutual position in the family life, beliefs that go unchallenged by everyone involved in spite of the reality distortions which they may continuously imply. The distortions occur as the family myth tries to explain the behavior of the individuals in the family while it hides its motives by substantiating a whole different set of reasons, motives and causes for the real ones.[1]

Family systems thus function in a way that is determined to keep the group in balance, and the family myth plays a defensive role as it protects its members from thoughts and feelings that may threaten that balance. In order to maintain the myth, certain distortions of reality occur in the beliefs of the individual members of the family. There is a subtle interplay between each individual member's defenses and the mutual defenses of the family system. These prevailing myths can sometimes then interfere with or even derail individual efforts at the completion of developmental tasks. For the myth to be dispelled at least one member must discredit it and behave in a manner that no longer supports it.

An example of a powerful family myth in action is the process we frequently see in families where a member is addicted to alcohol. In one family, mother starts drinking at three-thirty in the afternoon, just after the children return from school to "calm her nerves" because of their constant fighting. Father, who frequently works late, finds her sound asleep (or "out cold") in front of the TV when he returns at nine o'clock at night. He "knows" it is tiring to care for three bickering children. Thus, mother avoids her anger at her children and resentment of her absent husband by drinking, father avoids her resentment by denying her drinking, and the children detour marital conflict by acting up with each other. The family myth is that mother's drinking is "no problem." The distortions of reality that are required to support the myth are the beliefs that there is nothing amiss with mother or the marriage and that it is the children who are the problem. Every member contributes to the belief, including the children, and the parents may refer a child for psychotherapy. For the myth to be dispelled, as Ferreira suggested, at least one member must discredit it and behave differently. In the family in our example, the myth was confronted when 10-year-old Jimmy said, barely audibly, in a family therapy session, "I wish Mommy would stop drinking." This enabled the other children to express similar feelings, thus forcing their mother and father to confront the drinking and, ultimately, the problems in their marital relationship. Each family member became aware of his or her own vulnerabilities and, as a result, had the opportunity to contribute to the development of a healthier system based on realities rather than mutually protective distortions.

We have already observed the ways in which being a member of the adoption circle increases vulnerability to lowered self-esteem. The need to defend against this vulnerability would quite naturally encourage efforts to protect the individual's and the family's sense of balance and integrity. Let us look at the kinds of myths and dynamics these efforts may prompt in the adoption circle.

LOSS AND ANGER

As discussed earlier, the adoption circle derives from losses experienced by each of its members that may contribute to lowered self-esteem. Birth parents lose their biological offspring; adoptive parents lose the experience of bearing their own children; adoptees lose the opportunity to be borne and raised by the same parents. These losses are distressing for each in his or her own way. At times, each member reminds the other of the loss. The loss is, of course, balanced by gains: birth parents gain the freedom from a premature childrearing responsibility and sometimes a social stigma, adoptive parents gain the opportunity to love and raise a child, adoptees gain a ready family. Each person weighs the losses against the gains over time.

Associated with the loss of natural biological relationships are a sense of loss of normal status and, sometimes, feelings of helplessness. For the child—and perhaps for the adoptive parents and birth parents, too (depending on their previous life experiences)—acknowledgment of the need for an adoption signals a loss of innocence. The childlike belief that the world is fair, predictable, and trustworthy is dispelled. Instead, there develops a lifelong struggle to cope with the reality of this alternative family structure and the need to understand why it had to be this way. Each member of the circle struggles with continuing feelings of helplessness. Children simply get placed by powerful adults. Adoptive parents must submit themselves to the powers of adoption agencies, lawyers, and birth parents. Birth parents are subject to comply with the existing social and legal system. Each member is required to engage in experiences that are different from those leading to the formation of the "normal" nuclear family and to deal with continuing societal ambivalence toward this kind of family formation that is seen by everyone as less preferred.

It is natural for feelings of helplessness to produce anger and aggressive behavior. This phenomenon is often referred to as "helpless rage" in the literature on human behavior. "I shouldn't have to give up my baby" a birth mother insists. "I want to have my own baby," demands an adoptive mother. "Why do I have to be adopted—why can't I be 'regular' like the other kids?" an adoptee complains. Anyone in a position of helplessness must find ways of dealing with this anger and modulating the aggressive behavior it prompts.

When there is a sense that something unfair or "bad" has happened, it is common for people to ascribe guilt or blame for the event. The anger related to helplessness can, in this way, find a target by being directed at others, in blaming them, or by being directed against oneself, by assuming responsibility and feeling guilty. In their ambivalence and confusion, some people will move back and forth between guilt and blame. This shifting can occur over a single incident and/or can occur over the course of a lifetime. There may be times when the expression of such feelings seems unmodulated and out of control while at other times the expression may seem overcontrolled. Members of the adoption circle will struggle with their own feelings of loss and anger as well as the expression of these feelings by other members.

A common and often overriding way for adoption circle members to deal with the loss of control over their own lives, the loss of the biological relationship, and the loss of normal status is to rely on the powerful defense of denial and to attempt to enlist significant others to collude in this denial. Adoptive parents may attempt to prove to themselves that this child is theirs alone and that there is no difference between this family and any other. To protect themselves from the pain of the rejection and the shame of being relinquished, the adopted child may readily agree with the parents' beliefs. Adoptive parents may insist, "This is my child, whom I diapered, fed, and nursed when sick. Real parents are the ones who do the raising." Their child colludes with the belief: "These are my real parents because they take care of me. I don't have to think about birth parents because they didn't do anything but give birth to me." Absent birth parents tactically participate by remaining unknown and thus perpetuating the ongoing myth that this family is "just the same" as a biologically derived family. If adoption is "just the same," there is no reason to be angry out of disappointment or shame. As long as none of the players challenges this set of beliefs, the myth prevails. At the same time, however, the very feelings that are being denied can emerge and challenge the prevailing myth. Let us look at some of the ways this can happen.

The initial placement of the child would appear to be one couple's loss and another's gain, and in some ways this is true. The relinquishing couple loses the actual daily presence of their child while the adopting couple gains possession of a child for whom they have longed. At the same time, there may be mutual envy and feelings of inadequacy since each couple is unable to do what the other can do. As they view each other (or simply think about each other), their feelings of loss, compounded by a sense of incompetency, are heightened. Each person will want to find ways of avoiding or diminishing these painful feelings. One way of avoiding them is to try to keep the painful reminders at a distance, in fantasy and in reality. Thus, an effort may be made to keep thoughts of the other out of the house. In birth families there may be an unspoken rule that the adoptive family is not to be thought about, much less mentioned. Similarly, there may be clear messages given in the adoptive home that expressing thoughts and feelings about birth parents is out of bounds.

One way of diminishing feelings about incompetency is to devalue the competitor. Birth parents may discredit adoptive parents' strengths by attributing them solely to the external resources, such as money or education, that they themselves lack. Adoptive parents may similarly defend their sense of competency by devaluing the birth parents' ability to conceive and give birth to a healthy child by placing these functions outside the purview of "real" parenthood. And, of course, the "safe distance" required to avoid and diminish these painful feelings of incompetency precludes participation in search and reunion activities.

When the child becomes aware of his or her adoptive status, there begins a reflecting back and forth between adoptive parent and child as they process the salient issues. Directly and behaviorally, in words and music, they ask and answer each other's questions about their status. "Am I here for good, or am I going to be abandoned again?" a child may ask in many ways. We have already seen how this question often takes the form of behavior that tests adoptive parents' limits and commitment. "Are you here for good or are you going to turn your back on us and leave us one day?" parents want to know (this is a question that comes into sharp focus for many adoptive parents when their children express interest in searching).

Sometimes the anxieties of different members of the circle converge. Adoptive parents may in some ways believe that they are not entitled to keep the child permanently. When they have not fully claimed their child, parents may feel guilty for experiencing the joy of which the birth parent has been deprived. "If she knew what a wonderful child he is, she would never have given him away. If she knew now, she would surely want him back. Though I know we did this thoughtfully and legally, I sometimes feel like a kidnapper," said one adoptive mother who, in her heart of hearts, felt that this wonderful child really belonged to his birth mother. And that child himself, struggling with feelings of rejection and abandonment, may be questioning his belongingness. Thus, parent and child may converge in the underlying belief that they are not entitled to each other. Parents with unresolved fertility issues may think of themselves as damaged, inadequate, and thus undeserving of this lovely child, and a child who feels like the bad seed of a good birth mother may not feel entitled to good adoptive parents. In their behavior, parents and child may desperately ask each other, again and again. "Do you really want me? Do you want me more than you want your own flesh and blood?" (This question may be of particular concern for the adoptee whose parents have their own biological child.)

Adoptive parents and children may also push each other's limits to answer these poignant questions. When there are these complementary doubts festering, an escalation of anxious behavior on both sides readily occurs. A child's provocative testing behavior asks, "Do you (really) want me?" but adoptive parents may experience the test as a devaluing and rejection of themselves, thinking, "You must not love us or want us if you behave this way toward us." The mutual belief in lack of permanency in the relationship can well produce a premature separation. "I'll go since they don't really want me," thinks the child; "Let him go since he doesn't really want us," is the complementary thinking that contributes to what was mutually believed to be a predestined loss. Parents and child unconsciously agree that the family was not meant to be and participate in its disruption.

Meanwhile, adoptees and relinquishing parents have their own unfinished business of loss. Children—adopted or not—often entertain romantic fantasies of having been snatched from idealized birth parents who still continue to search and long for them. They wait and hope that someday a perfect parent will appear or that they will miraculously find them themselves. Imagining the perfect parent eases the normal everyday disappointments children experience in their parents. Adopted children must deal with some interferences with this idealized, comforting fantasy since they may have competing fantasies based on bits of information shared with them about their actual birth parents. And some of these fantasies are not so romantic: children may imagine birth parents as people whose lives they would have ruined—or still could ruin if they were returned to them. Children are bewildered by the knowledge of their relinquishment and struggle to make sense of such an event. They become entangled in a web of guilt and blame with silent or overt accusations of themselves and others. Each adoption circle member is "bad" or "punishable" at different times on different grounds, depending on the child's current circumstances and developmental stage. For example, there may be times when adoptees are absolutely convinced that they were kidnapped or bought by the adoptive parents and therefore blame them entirely for the separation from the idealized birth parents. At other times children may cite birth parents' inadequacy, irresponsibility, or downright "badness" for their fate. And then, sometimes underlying this blame and sometimes alternating with it, there is the sense of guilt of the children, who hold themselves responsible for the relinquishment. "Surely no good baby would have been given away," they think. "How could this have happened?" they demand to know. Each explanation through guilt or blame elicits anger at someone. Anger at the absent relinquishing parents can be maintained toward the fantasy developed of them or can be displaced onto adoptive parents, who are real and more convenient objects. Anger at oneself becomes a sense of guilt, sometimes leading to self-punishment. Blame of adoptive parents can be expressed through anger over everyday events. Thus, through the expression of guilt and blame adopted children attempt to explain their bewildering sensations.

Birth parents and adoptive parents also attempt to make sense of how this unusual and sometimes painful arrangement happened (to them). They, too, struggle with guilt and blame, which is expressed within the circle at different points in their own and the family's development. For example, adoptive parents directly and indirectly offer their own beliefs or interpretations of relinquishing parents' behavior: "If she wanted you, she wouldn't have given you away in the first place"; "If she wanted to find you, she would have done it by now"; "Maybe she has tried to find you and hasn't been able to"; "She may be hoping you will search for her."

Relinquishing parents also experience a range of fantasies and beliefs involving guilt and blame. "She is probably just fine with her good adoptive family; she wouldn't want me butting in—I would only mess it up for her. I've already made her life tough enough," says one birth mother in her guilt. Another says, with a sense of indignant blame, "I know she wonders about me as I do about her. I will no longer let these people (adoptive parents, social workers, judges, my own family) keep me from her. I need to find her so that we can restore each other."

An example of a colluding myth among all parties would be the relinquishing parents' belief that the child is better off without them, the child's belief that he or she would wreck their lives if contact were made, and the myth behind the following message from the adoptive parents to the child: "If she wanted you, she would not have given you away." With these common negative beliefs, it is difficult for each to realistically understand and empathize with the other's circumstances.

Accepting one's own and others' losses paves the way for being able to appreciate and enjoy the very real gains of the adoption family circle. Members can each come to take satisfaction and pleasure in the advantages of the alternative family for themselves and even to feel satisfaction that others' needs are being met.

ATTACHMENT AND SEPARATION

Struggles with attachment and separation are part of the normal developmental course for all people. We attach to our parents and separate from them; we attach to mates and sometimes separate from them; we attach to our children and, again, separate from them. For members of the adoption circle, separation and attachment are especially complicated by their common experience of loss.

As we have noted, relinquishing parents experience loss of their child and grieve in various ways with varying intensity from the pregnancy on. The way in which they separate from the child interrelates with the opportunity and quality of the adoptive parents' attachment to the child and then to his or her attachment to them. In the best of all worlds, placement of a child occurs in a time frame that provides an optimal opportunity for the child to attach to the new family. In such ideal circumstances, relinquishing parents go through the necessary agonizing struggle and achieve sufficient resolution for the child to have to endure only one shift of environment and for this to occur shortly after birth. Knowledge that the birth parents achieved some sense of peace about their decision contributes to the adoptive parents' tranquility as well. Again, in this ideal circumstance, adoptive parents would have come to terms with their infertility sufficiently to be genuinely open and welcoming of their nonbiological child. They would have had experiences with social and legal agents of the adoption that made them feel understood, supported, and trusting. With all these elements in place, there is a pervasive sense on all sides that this circle was formed for the greatest good and thus was "meant to be."

In our nonideal world we know that relinquishing parents' conflicts about the separation and impending loss will be reflected in the age of the child at placement and in the span, smoothness, and consistency of the process of the adoption. Ambivalent birth parents may need to postpone their decision. They may feel unable to take any steps prior to the birth and then may continue to put off a decision, hoping that time will help resolve their conflict; it often happens, instead, that the contact with the child that time allows makes a decision even more difficult. There may be many starts and stops in this process—sometimes involving contact with potential adoptive parents.

For adoptive parents, receiving a child as soon after birth as possible and the predictability and efficiency of the adoption process make a positive attachment more likely. If they are waiting, guessing, hoping, and experiencing disappointments, their readiness to open themselves up to a child is likely to be compromised.

The diminished availability of children for adoption in recent years has required potential adoptive parents to go far and wide in their searches. Compared with efforts involving traditional agency adoptions, these excursions tend more frequently to culminate in an incompleted adoption. Couples frequently describe these experiences as akin to stillbirths or miscarriages because they go through a similar kind of grieving for the child they fantasized about or perhaps even met, held, or took home. They may question whether they can bear to take the risk of another loss and, like biological parents who go through a stillbirth or miscarriage, experience a sense of inadequacy. In this process there can be a convergence of relinquishing parents' belief that they cannot or should not give the child up and adoptive parents' convictions that they were not meant to be or are not entitled to be parents.

While one research group found no differences in the quality of mother–infant attachment between adoptive and nonadoptive pairs, there can clearly be circumstances in either or both groups that might contribute to insecurities in these developing relationships.[2] When the placement process has been shaky and adoptive parents feel emotionally guarded or when the child is unsettled by multiple moves, it is more difficult for there to be an early secure attachment. It may take longer for adoptive parents and child to give themselves to one another. Sometimes the lack of synchrony or mutuality in their readiness causes one or the other to resist the attachment. Eagerly awaiting adoptive parents may feel rebuffed by an unsettled child who seems inconsolable and unable to respond to their efforts at nurturance. This experience can stir issues of vulnerability. They may feel that their worst fears of not being adequate parents are true, a feeling that may trigger underlying concerns that the child does not and should not belong to them. They may dig themselves deeper and deeper into this trench and, as a consequence, be unable to respond to the child's overtures. The child then feels rebuffed and withdraws. In the most extreme cases parent and child may never really open themselves to a permanent bonding. It is as if they internally decide that never again will they place themselves in the position of suffering so profound a loss. In these cases the image of the birth parents casts a long and dark shadow over the newly forming family, and this image serves to stand between the new unions.

Even in those situations where early bonding and attachment proceed well, issues of separation will be complicated by the original loss, a fact that is a hallmark of adoptive family life. Normal, expectable moves toward independence, even in toddlerhood, may be fraught with fears by adoptive parents that separation means rejection. An adoptive parents' private response to the toddler's "No!" or "I do it myself" may be, "He doesn't really love me; he wishes I were another, more perfect, parent." Strivings toward independence that occur in developmentally appropriate ways may continue to stir up feelings of inadequacy in parents and be processed as criticism and rejection. With the child's increasing awareness of his adoptive status may come his own insecurities about distance and permanence. Thus, the anxieties of parent and child may interact with each other and interfere with the development of comfort and safety in the relationship. The more the parent may worry about measuring up as a parent, the more the child may demand that the parent measure up to the idealized, romanticized image. Parent and child can become involved in a futile dance that denies the genuine bonds built on the basis of the shared experiences of daily life. Again, without recognition, the shadow of the birth parent casts its dark influence.

To disrupt this impasse, parents need to have some experience that makes them question how they developed the belief that they had to be perfect parents; they need to move on from that impossible demand of themselves. Such a move delivers a message to adopted children that no parent can be expected to be perfect and forces them to question what is was that made them think they were entitled to a perfect parent. The futile dance can

then be replaced with the ordinary pleasures and woes of parent—child relationships.

The tumult of adolescence often produces expressions like
"You can't tell me what to do." The adopted child can expand
this to "You can't tell me what to do—you are not my real parents." Birth parents can once again emerge as romantic figures,
the "good guys" who wouldn't make such unreasonable demands. This phase of separation is often a time when adolescents
experience increased interest in birth parents, which may revive
adoptive parents' old fears of retrieval and feelings of inadequacy. In a way, the adolescent's fantasy is a reliving of the original abandonment and adoption with the parental figures reversed; that is, the child imagines he or she will be evicted by
adoptive parents and rescued by birth parents. Here we see the
collusion of individual fears and beliefs that can escalate into a
maladaptive cycle.

Separation during late adolescence carries with it greater complexities and vulnerabilities for the adopted child. Unlike their
nonadopted counterparts, adoptees have already been forced to
"leave home" once. This original leaving is the epitome of helplessness—an infant or young child physically moved out of one
home and into another. When an appropriate time for leaving
home arrives, the adoptee will be operating on his or her own
version of the original story, which may or may not be confirmed
by parents or significant others. If the original move was seen by
all as a benevolent one involving caring parties, this second leaving may carry with it only the ordinary Sturm und Drang of adolescence.

Despite their conscious wishes to have a normal family and
normal family separations, the mutuality of the underlying fantasies of adoptive family members may activate each member's
need to undo the bad deed. Adoptees may exert intense control,
this time ensuring their own power of entry and exit. Deferring
parents may collude with the child as a way of giving back to the
world the child they feel they unjustly held. In desperate moments, they may even fantasize returning the child to the birth
parents: consciously, they may wish to give the difficult child
back to let them take care of him; unconsciously, they may be
making restitution.

Another example of the effect of mutual underlying fantasies
on separation during late adolescence involves the belief that the
adoption occurred as a result of an irresponsible or unloving

abandonment. That is, both the adoptee and the parents share a belief that the birth mother relinquished the child because she did not love him or her. Leaving home now can replicate the original fantasy. Adoptees can make themselves most unlovable, thus provoking parents to want to expel them and fulfilling their own phophecy. The question they have asked each other so many times in so many ways over the years—"Is this relationship permanent?"—reemerges. During the moments following the child's provocative behavior neither can say yes. There may need to be many experiences of separation and renegotiation before such an answer feels true.

The issue of searches and reunions with birth parents is one that frequently comes into play in late adolescence and early adulthood. Some adoptees feel a strong need either to explore their backgrounds for information or to make contact with birth parents in order to answer some important questions for themselves. Birth parents may also become more active in searching at this time, feeling that they would now be less intrusive in the adoptive family and wishing to connect with the grown child. How each member of the circle processes the need to search will reflect their ongoing (real or fantasized) relationships and will have an impact upon future relationships. Some adoptive parents can understand their child's searching as a legitimate need and are able to support and aid in the child's efforts. It is unlikely that any adoptive parent will go through this experience without some discomfort or distress, but these parents do not use their discomfort to impugn their child's motivation and to equate it with rejection of or disappointment in them. Other parents may find the wish to search a threatening act of disloyalty and lack of appreciation. The implication for these parents is that the search means abandonment of them and "proves" the child's preference for the birth parents.

There will be varying responses for adoptees, birth parents, and adoptive parents when a search is completed. Some birth parents may immediately and unequivocally rebuff and reject the initiative for a reunion. Others may genuinely welcome this as a long-awaited, long-hoped-for event and wish to continue a relationship in some way. In between are those who respond ambivalently or inconsistently. Some families can successfully include relationships among everyone in the circle, others cannot.

Some combinations of individual responses are more problematic than others since they offer no checks and balances or disavowal of a prevailing myth. An example of such a myth is the combination of the provocative adolescent, evicting adoptive parents, and rebuffing birth parents. Here every member confirms the belief that no family is permanent since no one is able to function in a way that undermines that belief. The adoptee has verification that he or she will be rejected or abandoned, adoptive parents have verification that the child always wanted to return to his or her birth parents, and birth parents persist in the belief that this child would ruin their lives. The maintenance of these beliefs makes it impossible for participants to achieve a satisfactory balance of attachment and separation.

Another potentially troublesome combination is the searching child, threatened adoptive parents, and welcoming birth parents. The gratification observed in the reunion confirms the adoptive parents' fears that these birth parents are the parents the child would naturally prefer. They may emotionally withdraw, as if giving the child back to his or her rightful guardians. In such a situation birth parents may make up for lost time with their child, who now feels abandoned by the adoptive parents who have defensively disengaged themselves from the child. The dynamics of this newly formed circle interfere with the adoptee's attainment of mature independence. The power of the prevailing myths does not allow for the real and permanent connections an adopted child has with both his adoptive parents and his birth parents.

These descriptions of possible reunion scenarios is not meant to imply that searches and reunions cannot be successful. In fact, as more reunions are reported and studied, there is increasing evidence that the search is made for positive reasons and that there is a positive outcome for all members of the adoption circle.[3] Increasingly, such events are a natural part of the adoptive family life cycle.

Every member of the adoption circle experiences the lack of a genealogical line in which known biological relatives forge a continuous link from one generation to the next. While each member is lacking a different kind of link, what they have in common is that everyone is missing something. There are some ways in which these deprivations interrelate. One area of interrelationship is around the ability to reproduce successfully. Mentioned earlier was adoptive parents' possible envy of birth parents' ability to reproduce seemingly effortlessly. So may there be envy of adopted children who are able to reproduce and have in their lives an experience the adoptive parents have been denied. The wish for this experience may be partially or quite fully met through identification with the adoptee as the latter becomes a biological parent.

At the same time, the experience of reproduction may stir up the adoptee's interest in his or her genealogy. There may be medical questions about heredity related to the reproduction and also renewed interest in biological evolution: "Where did the red hair come from?" "Twins!—does this mean that perhaps I was a twin?" In some cases, it is the birth of a child that prompts an adoptee to search for further information or for the birth parents themselves. The colluding beliefs that may develop at such times stem from the adoptive parents' seeing themselves as inadequate and the adoptee's yearning for a biological parent to connect the generations. Despair of "Why can't I be a biological parent" is thus complemented with their child's lament "Why can't I have a biological parent." Parent and child reinforce each other's belief that the loss is irrevocable and without compensation. Each decides that it is impossible to transcend the loss. They may stay fixed in a position of distance and resentment that interferes with their ability to maximize the resources within and surrounding the relationship. If any involved party could begin to think and behave differently, the colluding belief—that this nonbiological family cannot function normally at this stage—could be dispelled. One possible shift would be for the adoptive parents to recognize how valuable they, as experienced parents, are to the adoptee who has just become a parent and to be actively supportive in their child's new role. With this shift, the adoptee can move out of his or her fixed position and accept the parents' help and closeness. With mutual empathy, they may be able to access the adoption records and secure information that will help bridge the genealogical gap.

Neither adoptive parents nor birth parents have progeny that they can see, hold, and imagine carrying on the family line. Adoptive parents' continuity is in the experience of upbringing that they have provided for their child; it is in the parts of themselves that they have shared and that are now reflected in who this child has become and what he or she now brings to the next generation. Adoptive parents may feel particularly warmed to see traditions and values carried on as an indication of family, if not genealogical, continuity.

Birth parents' sense of continuity rests in their provision of a biological beginning—and, if circumstances were such that they exercised control over the child's placement, in their efforts to guarantee their child an advantageous environment in the chosen adoptive home. Like all parents, they hope the child carries on the most positive aspects of the family genealogy. Whatever adult relationships the adoptee maintains with adoptive parents and birth parents, each set of parents is forever cut off from a part of the continuity of the child's life: adoptive parents can never be a part of the child's genetic inheritance and birth parents have had no part in the transmission of traditions and values. Each set of parents envies the other's experience and may also hold the other responsible if development goes amiss. But there is also often gratitude between members of the adoptive circle. Adoptive parents feel grateful to birth parents for producing the child, birth parents feel grateful to adoptive parents for providing a good home, and adoptees may feel grateful to both sets of parents when they feel they were provided with a good biological start *and* a good upbringing.

IDENTITY

We have already seen the ways in which being a member of an adoptive family circle profoundly affects one's sense of self. All members in their own way, struggle with what it means about them and to them to be a part of the circle. They also raise and answer these questions to each other over the years.

The first question members of the circle contend with is "Why did this happen?" And consequently: "What does it mean about me?" Birth parents may come to answer this question in a variety of ways. For example: "I was young and irresponsible"; "I was unlucky—birth control just didn't work for me"; "I was angry and acting out"; "I was an indecent person in every way, first by conceiving the child and then by giving her away." Adoptees answer this question for their birth parents also in a variety of ways: "She was a good lady, but I was a bad baby so she gave me away"; "She was a slut, but I was good so she gave me to a good family." Adoptive parents also have attitudes toward birth parents. They may agree with the child that the birth mother was a "slut," or they may agree with the child that he was a bad child and thus deserved to be given away. Indeed, they may have concerns about the character of those who would relinquish their own child.

Adoptive parents also question and answer to themselves

why reproductive problems happened to them. Some may feel their infertility is "God's will" that they take care of the needful child. Some may see it as punishment for a sexual transgression— or for any other thought or behavior about which they feel guilty—and may conclude that it means they are not deserving of biological parenthood. Some may see it as a random, undeserved happening.

Any of these beliefs of any of the members of the adoption circle are likely to become reinforced, and then sometimes solidified, when they are supported by another member of the circle. Each person struggles with feelings of self-esteem and self-valuing. For example, when children feel that they were "bad" and adoptive parents also experience them as troublesome in some way, the children are likely to incorporate this sense of being a "bad seed" or troublemaker into their identity. Such characteristics as a physical anomaly, hyperactivity, or a learning disorder can also contribute to a mutual sense of the child as "trouble." Similarly, children can hold adoptive parents responsible for whatever difficulties befall them and thus support their parents' feelings of inadequacy.

Sexual issues in the circle tend to be especially salient ones, and sexuality and reproduction sometimes become confused. Adoptive parents may retain a sense of sexual deficiency as part of their ongoing identity. Adoptees struggle with the consequences of their birth parents' sexuality and whether this means that they themselves are inherently sexually irresponsible. Adoptive parents may have the same question and may be overly vigilant or overreactive in relation to the child's emerging sexuality. The pubescent child, in turn, experiences the parent's anxiety and then has to wonder if there is truly something to worry about. This collusion of fears may contribute to a distorted sexual identity formation in the child.

It is equally possible that such questions about identity will be answered in a mutually supportive and corrective manner. Individuals can be seen as themselves and their issues appropriately differentiated from those of other adoption circle members. In this way, one helps the other deal with the paradoxes each faces.

The formation of an adoptive family system is based on paradoxical relationships and thus stirs up questions about who and what is "real" or authentic. Are birth parents or adoptive parents "real"? In what ways? Is the child "really" a member of the adoptive family? All participants are aware of aspects of themselves that are not as they present themselves to be to the world. Birth parents resume their lives as workers, spouses, and parents but with the knowledge that they relinquished a child, an unusual and profound experience. Adoptive parents raise their children with the same efforts as other parents but with the knowledge that, biologically, these are other people's children. Again, this is an unusual and profound experience. Children are raised with the knowledge of having different birth parents and nurturing parents, and spend a lifetime struggling with issues related to this fact. All participants harbor feelings about not being typical, usual, normal, or somehow the way they are "supposed to be."

The anxiety around authenticity can be expressed in many ways and may influence other adoption circle members' sense of themselves. Each has the opportunity to travel the range from denial through acceptance to insistence on differences, and each position may serve a different function at different times. All circle members face special tasks in reconciling themselves to the realities of their circumstances. In the process they may visit their internal conflicts upon each other. For example, children may be sensitive to not looking like or seeming like other members of their adoptive family. They may feel that they are not really a family member and may maintain a perception that they are a false representation. If, at the same time, adoptive parents are holding on to the wish for their idealized biological child, they confirm their child's sense of not being "right," of being false. They may go back and forth in confirming the inauthenticity of the family. Birth parents may become involved in the collusion by searching with the mind-set of claiming their "real" child.

It is also possible for members of the triad to confirm each other's sense of being different and real. This requires individual acceptance of the special development of the adoptive family system, with support for other members' unique tasks.

IMPLICATIONS OF SHARED THEMES

There is nothing unusual about the fact that family members have significant effects upon each other. This is true for all families. Other family systems, such as remarried families, also include nonblood parent–child relationships. All families also have their share of intergenerational myths that are perpetuated over time. The aspect of adoptive family life that can make it such a challenge is the depth and poignancy of the human issues its members must confront.

Each member of the circle has endured the deprivation of a normal human experience. This deprivation requires each participant to confront and master the vulnerabilities such a deprivation presents. The kind of vulnerability and how it unfolds in ensuing years will vary from person to person. However, for all involved, the common thread is deprivation, and each seeks ways to master it.

Psychologists tell us about individuals who have felt deprived of something important to them and how they come to feel entitled to having the loss made up to them, entitled to some compensation for the unfairness of the bad thing that has happened to them. If the wrong cannot be undone, they feel, it should at least be repaired.

Few of us ever really accept that the world can be unfair and that when things go wrong it is not necessarily anyone's fault. There are many ways in which members of the adoption circle sometimes hold themselves responsible for their ill fate or seek reassurance and comfort from others. In receiving these kinds of emotional supplies, there is an enhancement of self-esteem. Giving the victim of deprivation what he feels entitled to conveys the message "You are good; you need not suffer." In the process of receiving these emotional goods, the belief that one's badness was responsible for the ill fate diminishes.

Many receive this kind of support from within and from outside of the adoption circle. Adoptive parents can assure their children that they were good babies for whom an adoption plan was made out of love and concern. Children can reassure their adoptive parents of their love despite their wishes for their birth parents. Birth parents and adoptive parents can communicate respect and empathy for each other. Significant others—in familial, personal, and professional relationships—can surround the circle with approval, support it as a good, healthy solution for all involved, and recognize and empathize with the members' struggles. In fact, according to a recent study, adoptive parents and birth parents expressed empathy and support for each other and for the struggles of the child in a majority of cases.[4] Their responses on questionaires indicated that they "felt" for each other and were willing to act on behalf of each other and each other's needs. This study suggests that there may be less self-centeredness and fewer conflictual needs within the adoption circle than is commonly thought.

At the same time, we hear of support groups for adoptees, birth parents, and adoptive parents growing at rapid rates. What is observable in such groups is a palpable passion and a direct expression of members' sense of entitlement to having their deprivation repaired in some way. There is variation in the form of reparation demanded. Adoptees may simply want understanding and the opportunity to share the struggles in which they have felt alone. Some may want full nonidentifying information about the birth parents while others may want identification and reunion. Birth parents, too, seek varying kinds of reparation. Some wish only to be understood and accepted, some want protection of their privacy, some want information about their child, and some want identification, reunion, and contact with the child; some even want the child returned to them. Like other members of the circle, adoptive parents express a range of needs that they feel will repair the deprivation they, too, have suffered. Some express a need for the world to see their family as just the same as biological families, as a way of making up for the way it is painfully different. Some acknowledge the differences but need for their children to value them in a way that makes up for the lack of biological kinship; this valuing may include an element of loyalty and commitment that denies the existence of birth parents. They may also need for their children to turn out as well as or better than their fantasized biological children.

The content or form of the reparation varies within the representative groups as well as between them. One group can come to blame the other (or other interested agents) for the damage done and may demand that they undo it. The passion behind the demand reflects the intensity of the sense of entitlement, which, in turn, reflects the degree of deprivation felt. All members of the adoption circle struggle within themselves and with each other to achieve mastery over the painful circumstances of their lives.

CHAPTER 6

WHEN HELP IS NEEDED

Implications for Clinical Interventions

MEMBERS OF THE ADOPTION CIRCLE OFTEN NEED and request clinical services at different points along their developmental courses. This help may come from discussion groups, support groups, or individual counseling. When individuals, couples, or families find themselves stuck in their own suffering, or in causing others concern, a psychotherapeutic intervention may be sought. It becomes necessary to seek more specific help outside the family system when family members have tried their best to solve their problems with insufficient results.

Sometimes the presenting problem for people who are members, or eventually become members, of the adoption circle is adoption-focused and sometimes it is not. A pregnant teenager comes in to discuss whether to relinquish or keep her baby. A couple who has discovered they are infertile makes an appointment to discuss their marital problems. Adoptive parents refer their 13-year-old son because of problems in school. A family comes for help because their 15-year-old daughter and 17-year-old son, both adopted as infants, are in constant conflict with each other. A 60-year-old birth mother presents with depression

and expresses longings for her relinquished son. Each referral offers an opportunity for remediation of past or current dysfunction
and also for prevention of future difficulties. This chapter focuses
on interventions clinicians might employ. The following chapter
addresses primary preventions through the legal and social systems.

The previous chapters on the developmental tasks of birth
parents, adoptive parents, and adoptees and their interrelationships inform us of the possible impact that participation in the
adoption circle can have on development over the course of a lifetime.

For birth parents, unresolved issues of guilt, blame, and
shame and of separation and loss can interfere with ongoing developmental tasks. There may also be continued conflict in the
relationship with the other biological parent, whether or not the
two are married. There may be difficulties in establishing new
intimate relationships, and there may be overdetermined reasons
for producing and raising other children. Birth parents may need
help in reworking their unresolved conflicts. They also need to
be encouraged to accept the task of dealing with such issues as
part of a normal developmental course.

Adoptive parents struggle with issues around infertility, self-
esteem, and attachment to and separation from their children.
These issues may interfere with a sense of security in their relationships with their children and with the pleasures of parenting.
Adoptive parents may need help in addressing the challenges of
raising a nonbiological child.

Adoptees may need help in coming to terms with their relinquishment and with related losses dealing with trust and permanency in the adoptive home; they may be struggling with identifications and loyalties in order to ultimately understand and accept
themselves as people with different biological and rearing parents.

Birth parents, adoptive parents, and adoptees share common
themes of loss and anger, attachment and separation, and identities that involve paradoxical qualities. These common themes interrelate with each other in fantasy and reality over the life
course. There may be a collusion of beliefs, or family members
may challenge ongoing mythology at different points along the
way. Therapists thus need to understand both the individual client and the interactive aspects of clinical issues in the adoptive
family circle.

As clinicians attempt this task, they risk the danger of either exaggerating or minimizing the relevance of adoption issues. Historically, there has been a bias toward minimizing, which was based on the view of adoption as a perfect solution from which no special problems were expected. Today the majority of general clinicians are still uneducated regarding adoption issues. Many therapists, for example, receive referrals of adopted children who have been in intensive inpatient, outpatient, or residential treatment in which adoption and its related issues have never been raised in spite of the fact that the referring clinician knew that an adoption had occurred.

At the other extreme are clinicians who exaggerate the significance of adoption and view all feelings and behavior through an adoption lens. This is particularly true of some specialists who work primarily or exclusively with the adoption circle population and tend to become mired in a rigid view of their clients' experiences. Specialists in other clinical problems such as divorce, sexual abuse and alcoholism must, similarly, be on guard against an overly focused lens. A clinician well informed about adoption and all of its many complexities, however, can seek to understand the individual personality and lifelong developmental course of all participants, as well as the family and social systems to which they belong.

THE PROCESS OF CLINICAL ASSESSMENT AND TREATMENT IN THE ADOPTION CIRCLE

Clinical work in the adoption circle relies upon our basic understanding of individual and family dynamics and is informed by the particular issues that this alternative family structure creates. Thus, clinicians use their proven skills while taking into consideration the special tasks of members of the adoptive family system as well as the interrelationships among these tasks.

Most commonly, individuals rather than families are referred or refer themselves for help. The presentation may or may not include references to involvement in an adoption as a primary participant or as an extended family member. In general practice, a relationship to adoption is usually not mentioned immediately unless specifically asked for in intake material. Rather, it is likely to emerge, sometimes as an afterthought, in the assessment stage of clinical work. Occasionally, adoption remains a secret within an adoptive family. More frequently, relinquishment remains a secret in a birth parent's family of origin and procreation.

The manner in which the clinician deals with the facts surrounding adoptive relationships is critical and can offer an opportunity to the client for an immediate therapeutic effect. By responding to adoption information as a significant life event that is the result of everyone's effort at adaptation and coping, the therapist can both acknowledge the challenge and diminish the toxicity of the experience. In attitude and behavior the therapist says, "I understand that this is an important part of your life experience, one which I can help you through. It is not terrible and it is not wonderful. It simply is one of the important parts of the fabric of your life." Some clients will be immediately relieved that this aspect of their lives is being taken seriously. Others will feel relief in hearing that adoption is not necessarily a pathologically scarring event.

Assessment of the individual needs to include, but should not be exclusively based on, exploration of adoption-related issues. Clinicians need to collect the material that enables them to understand the personality and dynamics of this particular person and the ways in which adoption issues play a part. They thus need to examine the individual's personality structure, his or her place in the family system, and the family's place in its sociocultural environment. All of this needs to be done with a sense of where the individual and family fall developmentally.

Ideally, the clinician collects relevant data through individual and family interviews. When this is not possible, a genogram (a family tree with significant data about family history) and an ecogram (a diagram of community relationships) can also provide salient information and sometimes serve as therapeutic tools.

A common clinical presentation from the adoption circle is that of an acting-out adolescent adoptee and the distraught parents. Let us look at the technical aspects of the evaluation and treatment of such a case.

CASE ILLUSTRATIONS

Scott W., age 15, was referred to a child guidance clinic by his parents. The presenting problem, given over the phone by the mother, was her discovery of marijuana in the boy's drawer. Other recent behaviors of concern included lying and stealing from a local store. There had been long-term academic problems, and Scott was now "running with a bad crowd." Scott's mother described this behavior as uncharacteristic, noting that while her son had always been headstrong and willful, he had never been a real behavior problem; nor had he ever alienated himself from the family as he was now doing.

The therapist assigned to the case chose to see Scott alone first, hoping to establish an alliance with him. When his mother expressed concern about whether he would agree to come to the agency, the therapist called Scott directly; he reluctantly agreed to come in. Ms. W. transported her son to the first session, and Scott sat across from her in the waiting room. He was a handsome, well-built young man whose dress and demeanor gave no clue that he was related to the middle-class woman who had accompanied him. Scott reluctantly returned the therapist's greeting and handshake and belied his nonchalance with a questioning glance at his mother, who affirmed that she would be there when he was finished.

The therapist opened the session by describing the few facts she had about his parents' concerns. Scott began to sputter with righteous indignation about his mother's snooping in his drawer and his parents' nosiness. "They always want to know what is going on with me, and it's none of their business," he declared. He went on in a very typical adolescent mode, decrying middle-class adult values and extolling the virtues of his peer group, which appeared to be made up of poorly functioning teenagers of a lower social status than his family. He wasn't at all convinced that he wanted to follow his parents' educational and professional paths. Asked what kind of life he foresaw in his future, Scott described a working-class lifestyle that bore no resemblance to that of the family in which he was being raised.

The quality of this de-identification struck the therapist as going beyond the usual adolescent rebelliousness. She commented that Scott seemed to want to be very different from his family. To this comment he flared and exclaimed, "It is not that I *want* to be; I *am* different." After a moment of silence he added, "Why should I be like them? They are not even my parents." He then described how he had been adopted as a baby. Given encouragement, he explained that his birth mother was young, unmarried, and unable to care for him. He spun fantasies about her that were frozen in time as he described a still-young, well-meaning but irresponsible person with a working-class background. When asked about his birth father Scott looked blank, saying that he had never really thought about him. He imagined that his father had a strong build like his and that he perhaps had worked in construction.

Toward the end of this first session, the therapist commented that it seemed to her that Scott was in a kind of tough spot, that his images of his birth parents and his adoptive parents were very different, and that it must be particularly difficult because he has to guess about his birth parents and doesn't know much about them for sure. The therapist added that all teenagers had a job figuring out who they want to be and be like and that being adopted made it even more complicated. She noted that she had known other teenagers who were adopted and that little by little they had figured it out and could make real choices about what they wanted for themselves—apart from who their adoptive parents and birth parents were. At this point, Scott was staring at the floor and had softened. He said, "I never thought about it that way before." He accepted the therapist's request to meet with his family and scheduled another individual session so the therapist could get to know him better. The therapist's decision to meet with the family rather than with the parents alone was made in order to continue to foster an alliance with Scott.

In the family session the therapist was able to begin an alliance with Scott and also to deal with adoption issues in both a validating and normalizing manner. This set the stage for further exploration of the individual history, family dynamics, and social circumstances.

Scott's family included Ms. W., a 46-year-old elementary school teacher; his father, Mr. W., a 48-year-old engineer; and a younger sister, Jenny, 11. As the family entered the room for their session, the therapist was struck with how closely Jenny resembled her mother. Mr. W. and Scott took chairs (with Scott choosing the one closest to the therapist) while Jenny cuddled up next to her mother on the couch. The therapist opened the session by stating that she knew Mr. and Ms. W. were concerned about Scott and that she needed to get to know his family. Within a few minutes fireworks exploded.

Mr. W. complained of Scott's misbehavior, particularly his use of pot. Scott defended himself and attacked Ms. W.'s snooping, insisting on his constitutional right to privacy. He declared that he would continue to do whatever he wanted and that it was none of his parents' business. "It's our business as long as you live in our home," said his father. "So what are you going to do—

kick me out?'' Scott demanded. At this point Jenny burst into tears, and Ms. W. began sobbing; Mr. W. and Scott stared at the floor. The therapist allowed several moments of silence before commenting that Scott had asked his father a question and that Mr. W. had not yet answered. She said, ''Scott wants to know if you are going to kick him out.'' Still staring at the floor, Mr. W. replied, ''I don't know what to do anymore. Nothing seems to work. I'm afraid he is going down the drain.'' The therapist acknowledged Mr. W.'s frustration and worry but restated the question about kicking Scott out. Quietly, his father said, ''I don't want to kick him out; I want him to stay and be a responsible member of the family. We just can't live this way any more.'' The therapist directed the same question to Ms. W., who tearfully stated that she wanted Scott to stay, and then to Jenny, who warmly expressed her affection for her brother. The therapist then asked Scott if he believed them. ''I believe Jenny,'' he said, trying to hide his tears. ''Why not your parents?'' asked the therapist. Scott went on angrily to say that he did not think his parents really felt he belonged in the family, that he was too different. He felt they were constantly ''on his case'' and wanted him to be someone different from who he was. He said that his father wanted him to be an ''engineer-type'' and that he was never going to do that and was never going to be ''uptight middle class'' like them, either.

Both parents then took issue with Scott's ideas of their expectations, stating that they wanted him to be whatever he wanted for himself but that he had to meet certain basic standards of honesty and responsibility. Father added that Scott had many talents and could be a lot of things if he would only apply himself. Scott bristled and spoke of how he had heard ''apply yourself'' all his life and hated those words. They made him feel like he was not measuring up.

The therapist then redirected the session to the parents and asked if it were true that they had always been disappointed in Scott. This drew an affectionate ''no'' from them in unison. Ms. W. said Scott was a beautiful, cuddly, and spunky baby. He was a delight to everyone and for them a dream come true. ''A dream come true?'' asked the therapist. Ms. W. explained that Scott was adopted at two months; she and her husband were afraid they would never have children. There were no problems in the early years, and Scott even seemed to like having a baby sister. Jenny was one month old when they adopted her; Scott was then $4\frac{1}{2}$. They

felt the family had been a very happy one until the past year or
so. The only difficulties Scott had had were some learning problems in school. He had some trouble with reading and a great
struggle with math. He had received extra help for both, and
there was often tension in the house over his homework assign-
ments. Mr. W. agreed that the early years in the family had been
fine. Jenny talked about how she had always had fun with her
brother and indicated that they sometimes still had fun—but not
so much. She clearly adored her strong, handsome big brother.

When asked if he agreed with his parents' and sister's description of their family life, Scott said, "Yes and no." Yes, they
got along well and had a happy family, but he thought they were
always disappointed in his school work and never thought he
was good enough. Father inserted that they were always frus-
trated that he did not try harder because they knew he could do
better. Scott spewed a mocking "Apply yourself." At this point
the therapist made a tracking statement, saying, "Mom and Dad
think Scott can do a lot better academically if he tried; Scott is not
so sure he can or wants to and experiences his parents' concern
as disappointment and rejection." There was quiet assent in the
group.

The therapist next directed the discussion toward Jenny. She
appeared to be a rather easygoing, affectionate child, an average
student with no presenting problems. She seemed to have a particularly close relationship with her mother and looked remark-
ably like her, given that there was no biological connection. In
contrast, Scott looked nothing like Mr. W., who was of slight
build and of markedly different coloring. As time grew short, the
therapist made concluding statements. She said she could see
that this family had strong bonds that were established long ago
and that they all deeply cared for and about each other. She could
also see that the bond seemed insecure right now and that everyone was worried about what might happen to their family. The
situation was reminding her of other families she had known
where the children were adopted and seemed to have some special questions about whether the family connections were permanent if they did not have blood ties. These families had to find
ways of reassuring each other that they were family forever—
even through tough times like this. She said she did not know if
this was true for their family but it was something to think about.
The family all looked a bit unsettled by this comment but were
attentive to it. Another diagnostic session was scheduled, half of

which was intended for the whole family and half for the parents only.

The first family session could have been done in many effective ways. This particular therapist chose to focus first and last on the issue of the permanency of the family since it seemed to her the most palpable issue. She emphasized the positive attachments while noting but not exploring the real conflicts that would need to be dealt with in later treatment. In her concluding commentary she made the suggestion of a connection between the family difficulties and adoption issues but without an insistence, which would probably have been responded to defensively.

The second individual session with Scott occurred before the next family session. There was further focus on his learning problems, the diminishment of his self-esteem, and the way these problems made him feel like the "oddball" in his family. He saw his Mom and Dad as very close to each other and Jenny as especially close to Mom. When the therapist noted how much Jenny looked like her mother, Scott agreed. The therapist jokingly said, "Are you sure she's really adopted?" Scott smiled and said that he had often wondered about that, that it was eerie how much they looked alike. He added that he looked nothing like his dad: "Thank goodness; the guy has got no shoulders." The therapist wondered to herself what else Scott thought his father might be lacking, given the couple's infertility, but felt it was too soon to raise this question. The therapist did make the connection between Scott's feeling like the oddball in the family and needing to find others with whom to identify, birth parents being one possibility. Preparing for the next family session, Scott insisted that, in fact, he felt okay about the last one and also about the therapist seeing his parents alone.

The atmosphere at the beginning of the second family session was less angry but still intense. There was no response to the therapist's question about any reaction to the last session, and she did not pursue this further. Instead, she focused on gathering family history by using a genogram (see Figure 6–1). The parents first described their families of origin, with Scott and Jenny asking an occasional question or commenting on relatives they knew. Both parents' families seemed quite stable, with high values on education and achievement. Family togetherness was also highly prized, and there were regular gatherings and reunions. Ms. W., the youngest of four children, had been particularly close to her mother (now deceased), and everyone agreed that she was the

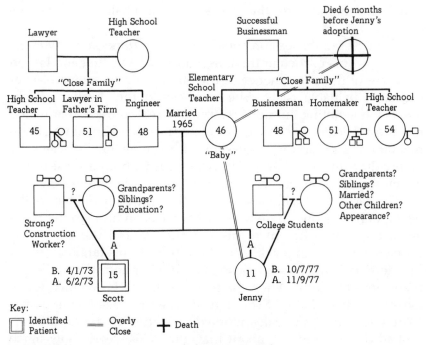

FIGURE 6–1 Genogram of the W. Family

The genogram form in McGoldrick and Gerson's standard text (1985) uses a dotted line for adoptive and foster relationships.[1] Adoption should be differentiated from fostering in its permanency. Thus, a solid line with an A (for adoption) is recommended. For some families, the dates of homecoming and legal adoption have significance and should be noted.

adored "baby" in her family. Mr. W. was a middle son. His older brother had joined their father's law firm, and his younger brother was a high school teacher, as was their mother. Mr. and Ms. W. met in their middle twenties, dated, and married two years later. They described always feeling comfortable with each other and sharing many interests and values. When asked about their plans and hopes for a family, they said they had both wanted three or four children and hoped their family would be close, like the ones they came from. They wanted to give their children opportunities for higher education. Scott looked physically uncomfortable, and the therapist commented that the fulfillment of that wish was a bit of a problem right now. Mr. W. added that he had had some hopes that his son would work with him.

"Like your brother and your father?" asked the therapist. Mr. W. shyly nodded.

There was then an exploration of the adoption of Scott and Jenny. The therapist did not, in the company of the children, ask any questions about the causes of the couple's infertility but instead pursued their efforts at adoption. Both were agency adoptions that went smoothly. Jenny asked questions about the procedures, and Scott wanted to know how much money they paid. The therapist in a playful tone asked Scott how much he thought he was worth. He smiled (for the first time in a family session) and assessed his worth at "twenty to thirty million dollars." Mr. W., also playfully, told Scott he hated to disappoint him but there was a standard fee for agency services, which was the same for all kids and only in the hundreds of dollars. At this point, the atmosphere relaxed more.

Having placed Scott and Jenny on the genogram, the therapist drew in Scott's birth parents and asked what he knew about them. "Not very much," he said. She asked some specific questions about age, education, and health, drawing on the information already gathered in the individual session with Scott. When Mr. and Ms. W. were asked, they said they could not add anything. Thus, many question marks were placed around the genogram symbols. A similar process occurred for Jenny, who was very uncomfortable with the questions. All she knew was that her parents were college students who were not ready to get married and have a baby. She didn't know if they ended up getting married or not. More question marks were placed on the genogram. Neither Scott nor Jenny acknowledged a wish to seek answers to these questions. Asked how they hoped their future would look on this genogram, Jenny said she wanted to be a kindergarten teacher and have a lot of kids. Scott said he did not know. He thought maybe he would get married, but not for a long time, and probably would work in construction and have kids later.

Observing the genogram, the therapist noted that there was a pattern of closeness between mothers and youngest daughters on Ms. W's side. Jenny's adoption occurred 6 months after Ms. W's mother's death and may have had special meaning to her in reestablishing a close mother–daughter relationship. The therapist wondered aloud if Mr. W. was a kind of oddball in his family since he did not share an occupation in common with a parent as did his brothers. Mr. W. looked wary but said, "I guess you could say that." Scott perked up at mention of the word *oddball,* indicating that he recognized the theme that had emerged in his individual session.

Scott and Jenny were excused from the session for the "over thirties only" group. They agreed with the parents that they would go out for a soda and meet them back at the car. A plan was made for a feedback session the following week.

The process of constructing the genogram offered a benign way of collecting sensitive data about the existence of the birth parents and also began a consideration of the influence of family patterns. It set the stage for later confronting the dynamics that contributed to Scott's acting-out behavior. Even in this session, it was possible that Scott began to see his mother's attachment to Jenny and his father's pressure on him for academic achievement as deriving from the family history. The therapist was curious to see how much of this the parents were absorbing.

Mr. and Mrs. W. visibly relaxed as the children exited. The therapist wondered about this, and Mr. W. commented, "This is tough." He said he was starting to think about things in a way he had never done before. "Engineers don't think like this," he joshed. Ms. W commented that she was finding this both taxing and relieving and that she was beginning to think this was more complicated than she had imagined. At the same time, she was feeling more hopeful since Scott was calmer and more reachable since his first session.

The therapist directed the discussion to learn more about Mr. and Ms. W., particularly in their parenting functioning. Both expressed great affection for Scott. Ms. W. expressed her gratitude for being able to adopt him. Mr. W. described the fun he had had with Scott in earlier years and the loss he was feeling with the current difficulties. The therapist asked how they had managed these behavior problems and learned that, in fact, the setting of limits and disciplining had been weak, inconsistent, and thus ineffective. When confronted with their lack of firmness, Mr. and Ms. W. had to agree and commented that their friends and Jenny tell them that they let Scott get away with too much. They admitted they did not know how to discipline very well and commented that Jenny was so easy it wasn't necessary for her. The therapist expressed her perplexity at their seeming inability to discipline their son: they were intelligent, strong, sensitive people; Ms. W. managed dozens of children in a classroom. Why was it so hard with Scott? The parents had no explanation. The therapist said she knew some adoptive parents who, in gratitude for being given their children, felt somewhat overprotective and had a hard time making them tow the mark when it was necessary. Could that be true of them? Ms. W. thought that might well be the case for her. Mr. W. didn't know but said they had been afraid that if they stood up to Scott, they might drive him away. The therapist wondered whether it might not be just the opposite, that the firm limits might mean to Scott that they wanted to keep him appropriately close. The parents looked at each other in dismay.

The therapist then asked about their infertility. After an uncomfortable moment of silence, Mr. W. stated that he had a low sperm count. Ms. W. added that it may have been due to her, too, since she had irregular periods (however, further questioning revealed that no dysfunction had been diagnosed in her). Mr. W. said the kids did not know about his sperm count and that he didn't want them to. The therapist asked if he was afraid this would be discussed in family sessions, and Mr. W. acknowledged that he was. The therapist supported boundaries around personal, adult matters, as indicated by the separate parent session. Because of Mr. W.'s obvious sensitivity and Ms. W.'s efforts to protect him, the therapist decided not to pursue discussion of Mr. W.'s infertility further at this time, though she thought it might have some contribution to his reluctance to set limits for his son. She commented only that sometimes feelings of long ago find their way into our current functioning.

The feedback session was designed to take place in three parts: time with the whole family together, time with parents alone, and time with Scott alone. The therapist began by saying she was only beginning to know the family and had some beginning ideas and recommendations that she would offer for their consideration. She said she saw the family as a very close one but despite the closeness there were some important matters they didn't understand about each other that were getting them into some trouble. The parents' strong wish to duplicate and improve upon their families of origin was making it hard for them to recognize their children's individual qualities. Referring to the genogram, she offered as an example the possiblity that Mr. W.'s wish to be part of a special father–son relationship like the one his father and brother enjoyed was putting undue pressure on Scott to develop skills he may not have an aptitude for or interest in. It was also possible that Ms. W.'s closeness with Jenny was her way of keeping alive her very gratifying relationship with her own mother. The therapist speculated that as Jenny got older and needed to separate, she would perhaps get caught in the bind of wanting to meet her mother's needs while needing to grow up and acknowledge her own needs. She added that all families struggle with these ongoing family patterns and that it was necessary to sort them out so that each member had real choices and did not get swept along by momentum.

The therapist said she thought Scott was in the toughest spot in the family right now and that was why he had been behaving in ways that were presenting difficulties. She thought Scott had suffered emotionally from his learning problem in ways that no one could guess because he compensated so well over the years. But Scott, like most kids with such problems, had come to think that there was really something deficient about himself, that he was a secret "loser," and this had made him feel bad about himself. He had joined forces with other kids he knew his parents thought of as "losers," and that was his way of communicating how he felt about himself. The therapist shared her observation that the family's intergenerational value on education and achievement further rubbed salt into Scott's wounds.

"Another fact of your family's life that bears attention is the fact of Scott and Jenny's adoption," she said. "In most important ways, your family is like biological families, living and loving and fighting and working on a daily basis. But there are some aspects of an adoptive family that require special attention. For example, it is a fact that Scott and Jenny have other, biological, parents, and it is perfectly natural that they would have thoughts and feelings about them. Particularly at Scott's age, when he is thinking about what kind of adulthood he wants, he has to think about who he looks like and who he will be like. Jenny is at an age where she might be thinking similarly. It is a coincidence that she looks so much like mother now and it has made it easier in some ways, but the questions are still the same and there are lots of them. Mom and Dad probably have some questions, too."

The therapist made a recommendation for a combination of individual sessions for Scott and family or parent sessions to help work out the kind of issues she described. Scott tossed around a few red herrings but was agreeable to regular sessions. Jenny and the parents were agreeable to family sessions. In a separate meeting with the parents to work out details they asked for help in establishing firm limits for Scott and agreed to draft a contract to work on with him in the next session.

The therapist met with Scott for a few moments to affirm the goals of the individual work relating to his internalized negative feelings. He alerted her to the possibility that at times he would not be able to make it to sessions, for example, when there was an important rock concert. The therapist said she would make every effort to be flexible in scheduling but told him that there might be times when he would not want to come because the things they were discussing were painful or because he was angry at her for something. She expressed the hope that through these tough times he would try extra hard to come and work things out.

The therapeutic arrangements in this case raise the question of the advisability of the same therapist seeing both an adolescent and the family. This particular therapist was accustomed to working in this way and preferred the firsthand experience with each segment of the treatment. In her initial experience with Scott, she judged that he would be able to maintain a treatment alliance with her and that the individual and family work would enhance each other. The traditional policy of confidentiality was provided for Scott, the exception being any indication of danger to himself or to others. The therapist was alert to the possible transference toward her as the birth mother, a mechanism that might involve both idealization and derogation.

The treatment of this family proceeded as recommended. Scott was seen weekly as was the family/parents. In the $1\frac{1}{2}$ years of work, Jenny and Scott were seen together for three sessions.

Scott's sessions focused primarily on his feeling of deficiency, secondary to learning problems, and the way feelings were processed in the family dynamics. He actively felt his father's disappointment and felt that father wished he were a male version of Jenny. He had long maintained the fantasy that Jenny was, in fact, their biological child and that they only said she was adopted to protect him. The belief that his birth mother had relinquished him because she knew he had a learning disability was also uncovered. In the course of the sessions Scott experienced increased curiosity about his birth parents and thought he might seek more information about them later. His relationship with the therapist was more intense than is common in 15-year-old boys. The transference was dealt with all along, but it became particularly salient during the termination phase, when Scott's behavior regressed significantly. The therapist noted that termination meant that she would exist but not be in contact with him, just as his birth mother exists but is not in contact with him.

The family sessions focused on the interactive issues among them. The therapist pointed out father's covert messages and pressures on his son, which he was gradually able to identify and control. Mother and Jenny established more appropriate distance, which allowed for more emotional contact between father and daughter, taking some heat off father's overinvestment in Scott. Jenny resonated to adoption issues raised by Scott, and the sibling sessions took place to encourage work on their mutual concerns. Parent sessions focused on interferences to parenting and some reworking of unresolved fertility conflicts. Mr. and Ms. W. were able to help each other give Scott and Jenny the parental guidance they needed.

Scott's relationships within the family and at school improved significantly early in treatment. However, his functioning in the community continued on a rocky course. Even as he began to change internally, it was difficult for him to shift peer groups and he struggled with the group's influence over him. He did respond to his parents' increased limit-setting effectiveness with him and behaviorally stayed within safe limits. The summer of his junior year he attended a local junior college program and developed an interest in forestry and conservation. With his parents' hearty support, he planned to pursue this program after graduation.

Four years later Mr. and Ms. W. returned to the therapist to discuss concerns about Jenny, who had developed into a voluptuous young woman. They were concerned about her developing sexuality and feared she would become pregnant.

Diagnostic sessions with Jenny revealed that she was struggling with conflicts around herself as a sexual person. Prior to puberty her resemblance to her adoptive mother allowed her to repress questions and concerns about her biological heritage. Her body was now very different from her adoptive mother's, and each view of it shocked Jenny into a confrontation with her roots. At the same time, Ms. W. lost Jenny as the image of her idealized biological daughter and was disappointed and confused in dealing with her daughter's emerging sexuality. As a part of exploring her identity, Jenny at times behaved as she imagined her birth mother had behaved. She alternated between responsible and irresponsible sexual behavior. She took chances at becoming pregnant, as she thought her birth mother had done. She defended and criticized herself at the same time she was defending and criticizing her birth mother. She was confused about whom she was like and had both fears and wishes of being like her birth mother.

Jenny was seen weekly, and her parents were seen monthly for a treatment period of four months. There were also three mother–daughter sessions. The focus of the treatment was to help Jenny discover who she was. As she examined her feelings and behavior, she came to see that she did not have to be the reincarnation of her birth mother or her adoptive mother's idealized child (both Jenny and Ms. W. moved on from that early strong but limiting attachment). At the end of treatment Jenny was in adequate control of her sexual behavior, and her parents were reassured about her controls.

Scott and Jenny had both been involved in risky behavior. Scott was on his way to getting suspended from school and was involved in some illegal activities. Jenny could easily have become pregnant or contracted a sexually transmitted disease. Had their parents not been as motivated and flexible as they were and had the therapist not been as informed of adoption issues and as technically skillful as she was, either of these adolescents might have ended up on an inpatient unit.

Because of their histories, any placement of adoptees outside of the home carries special issues and problems. Sometimes the adoptee's escalating behavior is an attempt to reenact the original relinquishment. There are some cases in which interpreting this phenomenon to the adoptee and the family can prevent hospitalization and retraumatization. There are other cases in which the dynamic is so powerful in the family system that placement is unavoidable. The adoptee can not get off a course of behavior that demands expulsion and/or the parents are determined to give back responsibility for the child. The adoptee reenacts being a bad throwaway baby; the adoptive parents reenact the birth parents' relinquishment by placing the child in an environment for others to care for him or her with no intention of resuming responsibility. There may be a conscious or unconscious wish by either the parents or the adoptee for birth parents to be called in to take over. There needs to be clarity about these wishes before an initiation of a search and reunion can be therapeutic.

Thus, in hospitalizations or residential treatment, therapists must work with their teams to deal with these special issues of

separation and abandonment in adoptees. Such issues are reflected not only in the kinds of relationships adoptees and their
families establish with staff and other patients but also in adoptees' patterns of running away and in the plans made for their
discharge. The crisis of the institutional placement can sometimes
produce a reworking of dynamics and a recontracting of the adoptive family relationships to reflect their permanency. Even when
such recontracting is achieved, adoption related issues are lifelong for members of the adoption circle and may require interventions at other points in adult life. This lifelong quality is
equally true for birth parents and is reflected in the case of Elizabeth M.

Ms. M. sought treatment for depression at age 48. She reported having struggled with depression on and off throughout
her life but had never sought treatment for it. She had currently
been feeling debilitated, had thought it might be due to impending menopause, and had consulted her gynecologist, who referred her on for psychiatric evaluation. Ms. M.'s history revealed
a highly troubled family of origin with an alcoholic father and a
depressed mother. She herself first married an alcoholic; she then
divorced him and went on to a happier marriage in which she
had three children. She was particularly attached to her oldest
child, Jonathan, who was about to leave home for college. She
was clearly feeling an exceptional intensity of loss around his
leaving. The overdetermined quality of this loss became understandable only in the sixth session when Ms. M., with great pain,
revealed that she had relinquished a baby boy for adoption when
she was 16. As she parted with Jonathan, she was reliving the
loss of her first baby, a loss she had not adequately mourned 32
years ago.

As the story unfolded, Ms. M. had been a depressed, troubled
teenager who fell madly in love with a football hero and let herself
become pregnant by him. In retrospect, she thought she did this
as a way of getting him to marry her so that she could get out of
an unhappy home. When he refused, she went into hiding at an
aunt's home and placed the baby for adoption. The grief she recalled was more related to losing the boyfriend than losing the
child. She had never told anyone else about the baby and had
tried not to think about him. Her treatment went on to focus on
the depression that first led up to the pregnancy and the depression that derived from the loss of the child.

Ms. M. had never told her husband or children about her first child and was not sure she ever would. Hearing about searches and reunions becoming more common, she had sometimes wished for such an event to make sure her son was okay. Her wishes did not include a desire to maintain further contact with him since she felt she still needed to protect herself and her family.

This case is another example of adoption circle issues being understood in the context of general development and personality organization. Ms. M.'s struggle with depression had begun early in her adolescence and was related to the deprivation of relationships with her parents. Her attachment to her football hero, with the resulting pregnancy, was an effort to compensate for this deprivation. Paradoxically, these attachments produced even further loss. It would be falling into the exaggeration bias to attribute Ms. M.'s depression entirely to the relinquishment of her child, but it would be falling into a minimizing bias to see the deprivations of her early life (or a possible endogenous depression) as the only salient factors.

SPECIAL FEATURES OF CLINICAL WORK IN ADOPTION

In recent years therapists have begun to address adoption issues in clinical work.[2,3,4,5] The remainder of this chapter summarizes some special features of this work.

Acknowledgment of the Circle

Assessment and treatment of any individual or subsystem of the adoption circle must be undertaken with an awareness of the circle as a whole and the ways in which its participants remain part of each other's worlds in fantasy or reality over the course of their lifetimes. No adoption circle member forgets about the existence of the other members. Participants need to be encouraged to allow and express thoughts and feelings about these significant people in their lives, who otherwise remain as ghostlike presences and thus may increasingly interfere with the mastery of developmental tasks.

There may be cases where supporting efforts at searching for birth parents or adoptees may be an important part of the therapeutic work. The treatment plan might then also include found members, if they need help in adjusting to each other.

Normalization of Special Tasks

An important part of the therapeutic approach is to normalize the special developmental tasks of adoption circle members. Recognizing that it is necessary and natural for them to deal with special issues lessens the feeling of abnormality and detoxifies the struggles. At the same time, it is important that the therapist respect the range of individual differences in confronting these tasks and not rigidly define normality and health. For example, the need to search was once seen as an indication of an unsuccessful adoption. In some quarters a lack of interest in searching is now seen as pathological denial. Adoption circle members may think, feel, and behave very differently as they successfully resolve common issues. The notion of the normality of their developmental tasks can be enhanced through support groups that focus on the threads of commonalty that are woven through the fabric of different family and life experiences.

Acceptance of the Need for Alternative Courses in Development

Associated with the concept of the normality of special tasks is acceptance of the fact that there is sometimes an alternative course in development. For example, before they can bear more children, birth parents may need to wait longer than their counterparts who never relinquished. Children who are adopted at an older age may need a strong holding environment that other children would find overly restrictive. Adopted children may not launch into adulthood as easily as their nonadopted friends since their issues around identity and separation are more complex. And searches and reunions, or some kind of contact between birth parent and adoptees over the years, may be part of the family life. Thus, it is natural that an alternative family structure would involve, at times, alternative courses of development.

Support of Healthy Defenses

Special developmental tasks and an alternative course of development does not imply that members of the adoption circle do not have the same basic needs as other individuals. Therapists have frequently observed the negative consequences of individual denial and family secrets. With such experience, it is easy for them to overlook the need for ordinary defenses that vary over time.

There is a natural ebb and flow in the salience and intensity of adoption issues for all involved. There are times when these issues are primary and must be addressed, but there are other times when individuals need to comfort themselves with a healthy degree of denial or the use of some other defense. The skillful therapist recognizes these needs as they emerge and supports them.

Management of Countertransference

The formation of an adoption circle involves important human and social issues such as the creation of life, responsiblity for children, and the needs and rights of adoptees, adoptive parents, and birth parents. The primacy of these issues will stir up a wide range of thoughts and feelings in the clinician that may threaten his or her clarity and effectiveness. These feelings must be recognized and managed in a way that allows for optimum assessment and treatment of a complicated and often highly charged clinical presentation.

Transference

The therapist working with the adoption circle may become a transference object for the feelings of a birth parent, adoptive parent, or an adoptee toward any of the cast of characters involved. He or she may be experienced as the social worker (especially if, in fact, he or she *is* a social worker by training) who gives and/or takes children away. He or she may, at times, be the overprotective adoptive parent or the rejecting birth parent. A common and powerful transference is the adoptee experiencing the therapist (even a male) as the birth mother. The therapist may at times be seen as the idealized birth mother who has (finally) arrived to rescue and tend to the adoptee. With a canceled session or vacation, the therapist may quickly become the abandoning one. Adoptive parents may reexperience competitive feelings with birth parents and see the therapist as the better parent. If not attended to, such transferences can seriously compromise, if not destroy, the treatment efforts. Proper interpretation, instead, can be highly productive and enhance the therapeutic outcome.

Termination

The profound losses experienced by all adoption circle members makes termination a crucial phase in treatment. This is a time when work on previous losses will be revisited and reexperienced. In saying good-bye to the therapist, clients are also saying good-bye to others who have been important forces in their lives. Therapists working in the adoption circle need to be sure to allow sufficient time and opportunity for this important work to be completed.

In summary, treatment of members of the adoption circle occurs at many possible points along the life cycle. To be effective, such treatment needs to be undertaken with an awareness of the functioning of that particular adoption circle, the possible impact membership in an adoption circle may have on the client, and the special tasks such membership requires. The therapist who is oriented and informed in this way is best able to use his or her established general skills to assist birth parents, adoptive parents, adoptees, and their extended families in their efforts at coping and adaptation.

CHAPTER 7

SURROUNDING THE ADOPTION CIRCLE

Implications for Social and Legal Practice

THE ADOPTIVE FAMILY IS a social structure developed for the care of children in need that meets the complementary needs of adoptive parents and birth parents. This social structure is as old as family life itself, with adoption arrangements historically made on an informal basis. Social and legal services for adoption circle members emerged over time with wide variations in practice and often accompanied by intense controversy both within and outside the adoption circle (see chapter 1 for a history). The intensity of the controversy is related to the complexity of personalities and circumstances involved in the creation of the circle.

It has become apparent through data collected scientifically, anecdotally, and observationally that participants in the adoption circle have a wide range of experiences. A common thread in all these experiences is the necessity of dealing with paradoxes. All participants must come to terms with the paradox of their biological and functional relationships: they are birth parents but not rearing parents, rearing parents but not birth parents, and children who are born of one set of parents and reared by another. We have seen that the confrontation with these realities results in stress for all members and requires them to find their own best modes of coping. These stresses have been cited by some as evidence of the inadequacy of traditional adoption as a social institution. There are many opinions about how these stresses may best be remedied or prevented. In looking back over the developmental tasks of each group of participants, we can see that some social and legal practices present problems to some members. Let us first note these problems. Later we will try to place them in context and consider alternatives.

PROBLEMS WITH SOCIAL AND LEGAL SYSTEMS

Birth Parents

Birth parents individually and in organizations have objected to some social and legal practices. Many feel that they were coerced into their decision to relinquish and maintain that had they been offered financial and emotional support, they would have been able to raise their child themselves. They blame opinionated social workers and families for forcing them into the belief that adoption was the best option for them and for their child. They blame overly solicitous doctors and lawyers for stressing the needs of potential adopting parents, and their own financial interests, over those of the birth parents. They cite a social structure that empowers those with financial and social resources. Some birth mothers say they accepted the idea that they would put the pain of the relinquishment behind them and go on with successful lives; instead, they have experienced a lifetime of grieving and regret. For those who remain committed to the relinquishment, some find that the practice of closed records has compromised their welfare and perhaps that of their child. In the hope of reducing their pain, many birth parents are now demanding an opening of adoption files. Some seek ongoing information about their child's welfare, some seek a reunion, and a few seek an actual retrieval of the child. Some are saying that social and legal procedures forced them into being birth parents and then made it more difficult for them to be birth parents who are not rearing parents.

Adoptive Parents

Adoptive parents cite social and legal interferences that begin as soon as they decide to pursue an adoption. They report confronting agency policies and practices that may immediately exclude them; they may live in a state where independent (non-agency) adoptions are illegal. Prospective adoptive parents have formed groups in some areas to help each other navigate what often seems like an impossible maze in the quest for a child.

Because the supply of available healthy young children is far below the demand, adopting parents find themselves in a highly competitive arena. If they compete through an agency, they need to prove their desirability according to the agency's values and, increasingly, according to birth parents' preferences. They must face the reality that if they do not agree with the values and practices of others, they may not receive a child. If they opt for an independent adoption within their own state, outside the state, or internationally, they must invest enormous time, energy, and money for a placement. They may experience a number of attempted adoptions that fall through at different stages of the adoption process, these being anything from simply having a child promised to having brought the child home. With each failure, there is a costly emotional and financial expenditure that some feel interfered with their readiness ultimately to attach to a child.

Like birth parents, adoptive parents complain that they were coerced by elements of the social and legal structure, that if they had not done what the agency felt was correct or what the independent facilitator required, they might not have achieved parenthood.

In past decades adoptive parents accepted the assertion that all any child needs is a good loving home to grow up as a happy, healthy person. Many even accepted older "special needs" children with this attitude. They now take agencies and independent facilitators to task for not providing adequate, sometimes crucial, background information and for not preparing them for meeting the special challenges and needs that are lifelong. In these ways, they feel the social and legal system has made it more difficult for them to be effective childrearing parents.

Adoptees

A lifelong task for adoptees is the integration of their biological heritage with their adoptive family experience. Many feel this process is made more difficult by the lack of information given to them about their birth parents and by lack of direct, or even indirect, contact with them. Some express profound feelings of helplessness as being the only ones in the adoption circle who had no say in the arrangement of this alternative family. Some blame birth parents for their abandonment and lack of contact with them. Some blame adoptive parents for withholding information or for procuring them to meet their own needs. Some blame social workers and lawyers for their presumptuousness in advocating adoption for unprepared parents.

Those who feel that additional information or contact with birth parents would enhance their efforts at integrity are demanding that their adoption files be opened to them so that they can make that decision for themselves. They feel that it is their right to have this information. Some would not intrude on a resistant birth parent whereas others feel it is their birth parents' moral responsibility to respond to their child's needs. Some await their adoptive parents' permission while others proceed without it.

Some adoptees feel that they need more knowledge of their birth parents to integrate two sets of parents. When they pursue their biological roots, they often face social and legal roadblocks and feel unaided in their quest. They feel that the closed record system deprives them of needed resources as they confront the paradoxes of their identity.

THE ADOPTION CONTEXT

Members of the adoption circle face special developmental tasks, as do families with other special circumstances such as divorce, remarriage, and chronic illness. We hear more about the problems such circumstances present than we hear about the ways people cope successfully. We have no survey research that can tell us what percentage of biological families cope successfully and are composed of happy, healthy people and no consensus on how such a measurement would be made. Nor do we have convincing research that tells us what percentage of adoption circle families cope successfully or that it is clear that participation in the institution of adoption is without a doubt superior to its alternatives—namely, raising a child when unready, being childless, or being raised by someone unprepared for parenting.

Even if we take the most optimistic view and assume that the great majority of adoption circle members cope as well as or better than biological families, we have to pay attention to what we hear about their struggles and what we hear from those who tell us there are aspects of this alternative family life that really do not work for them. As social and legal agents, it is our responsibility to reform our practices to enhance the quality of life for the people we serve. Let us now address our current policies and practices.

Current Understandings and Values

Practices regarding the care of children in need of homes have reflected social structures and values. These practices have also varied from state to state, from agency to agency, and between agencies and independent facilitators. Despite occasional efforts by the federal government and by national child welfare organizations to impose uniform standards, adoption practices remain largely determined by state laws and local customs. An effort is now under way by the National Conference of Commissioners on Uniform State Laws (NCCUSL) to draft a Uniform Adoption Act that would eventually be enacted, as a whole or in part, by all states and that would address our current lack of understanding of the diverse and, at times, problematic functions and consequences of adoption. A similar effort is under way through the Hague Conference to draft guidelines to govern international adoption. While laudable, these efforts are likely to be impeded by political and ideological controversies as well as by more reasonable disagreements about which policies will actually improve adoption practices.

What understandings emerge from our studies of the adoption family circle and from our general knowledge of children and family life that inform our recommendations for reform? A recent publication by Elizabeth Cole and Kathryn Donley lists and discusses the following ten values underlying adoption practice:[1]

1. Children are entitled to grow up within families. They need a safe, nurturing environment with at least one adult figure.[2]
2. If the family of origin is unable or unwilling to provide this experience, the child will need an alternative family.[3]
3. For children who need alternative families, adoption is the preferred mode of substitute parenting once it is determined that the child's birth parents are unable or unwilling to provide care.[4]
4. The adoption decision must be made early in a child's placement and with minimal delay and uncertainty.[5]

5. Adoption constitutes a lifelong experience for all parties (child, birth parents, and adoptive parents).[6]
6. Birth parents and adoptive parents should choose the degree and type of contract and information shared between them before and after the adoption.[7]
7. Adopted children are entitled to information about their birth, birth parents, significant genetic and social history, their placement, and the circumstances of their adoption.[8]
8. Information should be freely provided to adoptive parents so it can be communicated to youngsters during early childhood years in an age-appropriate manner.[9]
9. If adoptive parents refuse to give children information, the adopted person should have access to disclosure at legal majority.[10]
10. Preparation of adoptive parents should emphasize enhancing their parenting potential rather than investigating or rejecting them.[11]

These values primarily address the needs of children. As we have seen from our discussions in earlier chapters, in order for an adoption to be successful for children, the adoption system must be successful. The legal and social practices surrounding the adoption circle members thus must contribute to the well-being of all participants so that children can, in fact, be provided with a safe, nurturing environment.

Influences on the welfare of the adoptive system begin developing long before actual placement of the child. We have seen the ways in which adoptive parents' and birth parents' experiences in making the decision for an adoption profoundly affect the child's experience. Birth parents need to be able to make their own decisions about relinquishment and to grieve the loss of their child. They need to be realistic about what the loss means for them and to understand that they will need to confront the sequelae of this event, like any significant loss, in many ways over their lifetimes. They need to arrange an adoption plan that feels right for them and for their child.

Adopting parents need to grieve over their infertility and come to terms with the significance to them of the alternative of raising adopted, rather than biological, children. They need to recognize the challenges of adoptive parenting, understanding that *all* adoptees have special needs, and to decide if they are prepared to take on the necessary special tasks. Adoptive parents

need to have all available information about the child's background so that they can make as informed a choice as possible
about the kinds of risks they may be undertaking. They need to
be able to be honest with themselves in making an adoption plan
that they feel best allows them to provide for their child.

Birthparents' and adoptive parents' preparation for adoption
needs to be completed in a timely way so as to allow for placement with minimal delay and with a commitment to permanency
in order to be least disruptive to the child's sense of security. The
placement itself needs to be carried out in a manner that supports
all participants. Birth parents need comforting in their grieving;
adoptive parents and children need support in establishing their
new family. Older children may need extra help with the transition. Each family circle will have its own mechanisms for coping.
Some may want actual ceremonies; some may want more private
means.

It has become clear that adoption issues do not end with the
placement and that participants may need assistance in dealing
with these issues over the course of their lifetimes. Developmental issues of all parties require changes in the system. What
was adaptive in the early years may not work as well when individual needs and circumstances change. Thus, there may need to
be shifts in the way the adoption circle functions. As adoptees
confront the fact of the two families they belong to, they may
need additional information or contact with their birth parents.
Birth parents may also vary in their need for information and contact. As in all relationships, the boundaries between birth parents, adoptive parents, and adoptees need to be flexible over the
life course so as to accommodate changing needs.

IMPLICATIONS FOR POLICIES AND PRACTICES

It is much easier to state the need than to prescribe how the needs
can best be met, for, at times, there are conflicting needs and any
prescription values one need over another. Let us now consider
how the social and legal systems might best respond to the needs
we have described.[12]

Arrangement of the Adoption

Controversy has always swirled around the quality of services offered during adoptive placements. Informal or direct placement
of children with "strangers" by parents acting on their own or

with the assistance of facilitators has long characterized adoption practice in this country. All but five states (Connecticut, Delaware, Massachusetts, Michigan, and Minnesota) continue to permit independent placements, subject to varying degrees of regulation. Since the late 19th century the states have also licensed public and private agencies to supervise the placement of children with foster parents or adoptive parents. In the past decade agencies and independent facilitators have been criticized for their policies and practices. Agencies are most often criticized for the rigidity of their requirements, which they feel uphold rigorous standards devoted to the best interests of the child. Independent facilitators are most often criticized for their self-serving nature and their lack of knowledge and concern for anyone else's well-being. Independent facilitators challenge the beliefs and practices of local adoption agencies, and through their recruitment efforts are able to obtain more of the healthy white infants most adopting parents prefer. Publicized cases of mismanaged adoptions have occurred in both the agency and the independent sector; well-handled adoptions also occur in both sectors.

Given our knowledge that birth parents and potential adoptive parents represent a wide range of needs and circumstances, it is appropriate to provide both agency and independent services. Some birth parents and adopting parents will find comfort and support in the standards of their local agencies and will enjoy the protection such agencies can provide. Others may find some agency arrangements unworkable for them and will prefer an independent facilitator. They may not meet agency age requirements, for example (a long wait may exempt them), or may not feel comfortable with agency practices. Some prospective adopters and birth parents oppose the closed, secretive practices of traditional agencies and resort to independent placements in order to have a more open adoption. Others oppose the emphasis of some agencies on absolute and continuing openness and therefore turn to independent facilitators who can "guarantee" a confidential adoption. Thus, agency practices have encouraged the growth of independent placements.

Since all adoptions must be approved by the court, there is an established mechanism for upholding standards and practice for both agencies and private facilitators. This leads us to consider what standards of practice should be arranged in an adoption. In the days when children were considered tabula rasa, there was little interest in collecting data about their backgrounds, except for the few known hereditary diseases. Preadoption information gathered by agencies centered primarily on the adopting parents and the social psychological and economic environment they were likely to provide. With increasing evidence of biological components of development (genetic, prenatal, and postnatal), adoption facilitators and parents more highly value this information (as well as background information about older children available for adoption).

It is logical that the most knowledgeable and informed arrangement can be made when a great deal of information about birth parents, adoptive parents, and the child is available for exchange. We have also seen the ways in which adoptees need information about their birth parents as they grow up. Thus, the adoption agent would want to know all available medical, social, and psychological information about participants. However, the gathering of this information is complicated by the context in which it is gathered. Each participant has an agenda that may consciously or unconsciously compromise the provision of information. Birth parents want people they consider the best candidates to accept their children. They may feel that certain facts or features of their backgrounds or their families' backgrounds may deter such acceptance. Moreover, birth parents may not know much about themselves or their families and may not seek out more information. They may not have much of a medical history to report at the time of placement, but may have more to report in later years. Birth mothers may actually know little about the child's father or may withhold his identity or information about him to protect herself from his involvement. Thus, while birth mothers exercise their right to privacy, adopting parents may have access to limited information on which to base a decision for acceptance of a particular child.

Adopting parents want to be accepted by an agency or by the birth parent. They may fear that they will not compete well with other candidates if some aspects of their backgrounds are known and therefore may, consciously or unconsciously, withhold selected information. Thus, we see that at the moment in time when there is the best opportunity for sharing information, there are forces on both sides that interfere. In current practice, adoption agencies are required to gather and store information, but in most states private facilitators may not be required to do so. Many independent agents collect little information and may not keep a record of what they do collect. More states are becoming aware of the need for information, both for placement purposes and for sharing with adoptees in a timely manner, and many are now establishing an ongoing collection system so that birth parents can continue to communicate relevant facts (such as the emergence of possibly hereditary illnesses) after an adoption has been finalized.

The collection of data—for placement, for adoptees, or for updating—is not standardized. In order to achieve the goal of standardization, we need to develop questionnaires that solicit significant background information and to make a completed questionnaire a requirement before placement. At the same time, we need to do what we can to maximize openness in the context in which the material is gathered. Agents could be required to have specific training in the adoption process before they can be licensed. There also need to be sanctions against agencies or independent facilitators who neglect to share background information.

Preparing Birth Parents and Adopting Parents for Their Special Tasks and Those of Their Child

It is now clear from all available data that adoption as a perfect solution is a myth. Birth parents do not "put it all behind them," and relinquished child have needs that add special tasks for adoptive parenting. Since this is our current state of understanding, it is our responsibility to share this understanding with participants in adoption. Counseling thus needs to be provided to help birth parents and adopting parents confront this reality and make a more informed decision regarding the challenges they face. Birth parents need to confront the meaning of the relinquishment. Can they really let this child go and allow him or her to attach to and be raised by other parents? In what ways can they remain available to the child over time should he or she wish additional information or contact later in life? How can they manage this and meet the child's needs? Adopting parents need counseling to confront the reality that both they and the child will have some ongoing issues around the adoptive status, issues that at times will present special challenges. Do they have the strength to take on these challenges and the flexibility to allow the child to take whatever steps he or she may need to take to cope with having two families?

Such counseling should offer a balanced view of experiences

in adoption. That is, adoptive parents should be informed of the wide variety of adoption experiences, which range from an easy, uneventful course to a highly troubled one. More specifically, they may find, as many families do, that the raising of their adopted child is easy and pleasurable; the child fits into the family well, enjoys comfortable relationships, and develops without any significant difficulties. At the other extreme is the family for which the adoption of a particular child wreaks havoc. The child may arrive with various kinds of vulnerabilities or may be a particularly poor fit for this family (of course, this circumstance can occur in biological families as well, but it is particularly troublesome with the added issues of adoption). From their knowledge of themselves and their families, those interested in adopting can make a conscious decision about the potential risks and potential gratifications. They can also make a more informed decision about the kind of contract they wish to establish.

This kind of counseling would best occur in the preplacement stage and, in fact, is often now incorporated into agency programs; however, it is rarely available in independent adoptions. Court finalization remains the only possible guaranteed control, since placement occurs in most cases long before finalization. Courts could include a requirement for such counseling before finalization; this procedure would be less than ideal but better than no counseling at all.

Hopefully, serious efforts at realistically preparing all parties would prevent cases of wrong relinquishment or wrongful adoption, which cause everyone great pain and are severely disruptive to the children. Current figures indicate that 10%–15% of the adoptions of older children are revoked, and adoptive parents cite the lack of knowledge of previous serious behavior problems and their lack of preparedness as significant factors.

Establishing an Adoption Contract

From the 1920s until recent years, the adoption of infants was arranged with a contract of confidentiality. While there was some variation from state to state, information gathered about birth parents was usually placed under court seal, to be opened only with "good cause." It was rare that a court agreed that there was "good cause," even when there seemed to be compelling medical reasons to divulge the confidential information. The original birth certificate was modifed to appear as if the child had been born to the adoptive parents, thus giving the child a new legal identity. These practices were consistent with the belief that the adoptive family was just like a biological family and with the view that through relinquishment the birth mother was able to leave her past (transgressions) behind her.

We have already described the kinds of difficulties the practice of confidentiality has presented to some members of the adoption circle. Some birth parents, adoptive parents, and adoptees now want the general data that are in the adoptee's file and sometimes want identifying information that would enable them to search for each other. There is currently strong controversy surrounding the opening of these files. Let us look first at the state of practices related to the controversy and later go on to discuss possible modifications of the traditional confidential contract.

Access to Adoption Records

In every state adoptive parents and adoptees at the age of majority have the right to petition the court for nonidentifying information. However, this right is not well known, and procedures for exercising it tend to be complicated, confusing, and discouraging. Even when records are discovered, they are likely to include skimpy information on adoptions that occurred 18 to 20 years ago. The frustration on finding such little information contributes to the need to search for more completeness in closure.

Currently nearly 20 states have some version of a "passive" mutual consent registry for disclosure of identifying information. This has been a very recent development: in 1970 no state had such a provision. Mutual consent means that birth parents and adoptees who have reached the age of majority must register their wish for identifying information in the proper court, private agency, or state office. If both have registered, the information is given to both parties. These registries have not been widely publicized, and the procedures involved are often unwieldy and, consequently, discouraging. When a match is made, the reunion is carried out in an unsupervised manner and is considered a private matter.

At least 16 states have a more "active" registry system in which the state provides "discreet" inquiry for adoptees 18 and over, through an intermediary. The state intermediary consults the records and attempts to find the relinquishing parents. If successful, the intermediary asks the birth parent if he or she is willing to have contact with the relinquished child. If the answer is no, no further action can be taken. When it is yes, some counseling is provided for both parties in preparation for the reunion. Some states allow intermediaries other than those appointed by the state to explore searches. There are now private search groups and individuals who maintain independent search services, who report to a national registry of completed reunions; these intermediaries see themselves as more invested and more successful than their state-appointed counterparts.

Strongly opposed to the opening of files for identifying information is the National Committee for Adoption, based in Washington, D.C. This lobbying group opposes the opening of records in the interest of preserving birth mothers' anonymity. Other proponents of adoption over abortion also advocate continued confidentiality, and a new wave of religiously oriented maternity homes is developing to encourage this choice.

Outside of the adoption-rather-than-abortion movement, there is little opposition to mutually consensual releases of identifying information. To the surprise of many, the research findings so far indicate that the overwhelming majority of adoptive parents support their children's wishes to search, and the overwhelming majority of birth parents welcome their searching child.[13,14]

There is significantly more controversy and lack of clarity of the issues when only one party is interested in a reunion. Some adoptees feel that they have a right to identifying information despite their birth parent's insistence on their constitutional rights to privacy. Some interested parties believe that the adult adoptee's rights supersede all others whereas others consider all adult parties of equal privilege, meaning that disclosure requires mutual consent. The issue becomes even murkier in circumstances where biological parents whose rights were terminated seek access to their children.

The practice of intermediaries that has developed through grass roots search groups and seems the most reasonable solution to the sensitive problem of unlocking adoption files. Such intermediaries need training to develop skills and procedures that are respectful of the needs and rights of all parties involved. Currently, their practices include gentle persuasion, with the intermediary trying again periodically to retest the waters. Sometimes the reunion is flatly refused by a party and thus uncompleted.

Adoption Contracts Today

Today there is a wider range of adoption contracts. Confidential adoptions are still the prevailing mode but with some modifications. Given the history of changing state laws and practices regarding opening adoption files, birth parents and adoptive parents are no longer promised lifetime confidentiality. In some states at the time of relinquishment birth parents are asked to register their preferences for or against disclosure at the child's age of majority. From 1980 to 1990, of those birth parents in Michigan who registered their preference on disclosure, 80% said yes to disclosure while the remaining 20% retained the option to decide at a later time.

Most states now require agency and independent facilitators to collect and share the following nonidentifying information.

1. The date and place of adoptee's birth.
2. The age of the biological parents at the time of placement and a description of their general physical appearance.
3. The race, the city, and the religion of the biological parents.
4. The medical history of the biological parents and of the adoptee.
5. The type of termination of parental rights—whether voluntary or court-ordered.
6. The facts and circumstances relating to the adoption placement.
7. The age and sex of other children of the biological parents at the time of adoption.
8. The educational level of the birth parents, their occupation, interests, skills.
9. Any supplemental information about the medical and social condition of members of the biological family provided since the adoption was complete.

There is no standardized procedure for facilitating the continuing collection of data. The greatest resistance comes from those who see this continued input as interfering with birth parents' ability to let go of their child and with adoptive parents' and the child's need to attach to one another. Similar concerns emerge regarding more open adoption contracts. Openness in adoption follows a continuum. Three general groupings of adoption type fall along this continuum and are commonly referred to as fully disclosed, semi-open, and confidential. Variations occur within each group, which may place an adoption type closer to the extreme of fully disclosed or the extreme of strictly confidential.

We have already discussed confidential adoptions. In semi-open adoptions, the agency or independent facilitator serves as an intermediary and conduit of communications. Usually, the agreement includes exchanges of letters, photographs, and gifts. While adoptive parents and birth parents may or may not have met and may or not have identified themselves, they have made an agreement to have secondary contact only, once a placement is completed. The effectiveness of this arrangement depends both on the parties' ability to follow through as planned and the reliability of the intermediary, who really promises to provide services for the adoptee's entire lifetime.

In fully disclosed adoptions, birth parents and adoptees agree to share identifying information and make arrangements for the type of contact they will have in years to come. Some communicate directly (that is, no intermediary is involved), but avoid face-to-face contact. The greatest degree of openness involves family visits, with children even spending time with birth parents.

Recently, a recommendation was made by Pannor and Baran, authors of *The Adoption Triangle*, that a new category of adoption be formed.[15] These authors concluded that even open adoptions do not sufficiently relieve the pain of relinquishing parents or the emotional struggle of adoptees and that all previous forms of adoption should no longer be practiced. They advocate, instead, offering all possible financial and social support to birth parents to enable them to rear their child themselves. In those cases where parents are still unwilling or unable to raise their child, they suggest a guardianship arrangement whereby the birth parents would still remain the parents. Those who in previous arrangements would have become adoptive parents would now become guardians with full legal and financial responsibility for the child. There would be complete openness in the relationship, with visitations as mutually agreed upon.

There is only beginning to be research on the effectiveness of more open adoption arrangements. Agencies with such practices are reporting good results, but the very small numbers of subjects and the lack of longitudinal data make it impossible to assess its effects compared to other arrangements. At this point we are only in a position to note the possible benefits and risks.[16,17]

TABLE 7–1   Openness in Adoption

Possible Benefits	Possible Risks
Birth Parents	
Increased feelings of control over decision	Increased ambivalence and negative feelings toward adoptive parents, including jealousy
Satisfaction of caring for child by participating in choice of adoptive parents	Increased concern about welfare of the child if disappointed in adoptive parenting
Decreased anxiety at not knowing how child fares	Increased difficulty in "letting go" of child, thus interfering with attachment between child and adoptive parent
	More difficulty in using healthy defenses when necessary
Adoptive Parents	
Living more realistically with adoptive status	Feeling coerced into meeting birth parents' needs vs. adoptive family's needs
More realistic confrontation with child's origins	Anxiety about satisfying birth parents' preferences in child-rearing
More realistic communication to child about his origins	Ambivalence toward birth parents, including envy of their fertility
	Increased concern about biological origins if birth parents are functioning poorly
Positive feeling toward birth parents and communication of same to child	Anxiety about birth parents interfering with quality of adoptive parent–child relationship

Possible Benefits	Possible Risks
Adoptive Parents	
	Increased difficulty in using healthy defenses when necessary
Adoptees	
Increased sense of integrity as a function of knowledge of both sets of parents	Increased fear of birth parents' attempts to reclaim
More realistic sense of genetic heritage to aid identity formation	Increased loyalty issues in having to deal with both birth parents and adoptive parents in formative years
A positive image of birth parents as people who remain concerned	Difficulty establishing a primary bond with adoptive parents as birth parents are too present
Feelings of relinquishment rather than abandonment	Increased anxiety about permanency of adoptive relationship
	Increased difficulty in using healthy defenses when necessary

PROVIDING POST ADOPTION SERVICES

While we are not yet in a position to judge the relative merits of different forms of adoption, what is already clear is that no one arrangement is right for all adoption circles. Some may thrive in a completely disclosed adoption while others may thrive in a confidential one. Participants need to be given ample information and opportunity to assess the needs of the child and the ways they can best meet those needs. Some adopting parents may feel they cannot include the birth parent if they are to bond and claim the child. Others may find this quite possible. Some birth parents may find it impossible to remain in contact while others may find it impossible not to. Hopefully, adopting parents and birth parents can come to an agreement that they consider to be in the child's best interests and that is consonant with their own parenting abilities. The kind of pressures participants once felt around the establishment of confidential adoptions should not now be replaced with pressure toward any other particular kind of adoption.

As we become increasingly aware of the complexity of the decisions that birth parents and adoptive parents are required to make, we have to think about what kind of time frame is suitable to make these decisions and what period of revocation should be allowed. There is a general consensus that the child should be placed as early as possible in a permanent home. At the same time, birth parents may be involved in conflicts within themselves, with families, and with each other over the decision. Thus, there is sometimes a conflict between the child's need for the earliest possible placement and the birth parents' needs to resolve their own conflicts. States vary in the allowance of time for revocation. Traditionally, agencies protect adoptive parents and the child by placing the child only after the time allowance for revocation has expired. Placements made before formal consent are at risk for disruption. In California, where most independent adoptions take place, 5% are reversed before consent, most within the first week. Hopefully, in time, more active and informed counseling of birth parents prior to relinquishment will contribute to their having greater confidence in their decision and, thus, to fewer revocations.

Once the contract is established, the social and legal systems need to offer all possible protections and support to the new family structure. This includes direct services to birth parents, adoptive parents, and adoptees.

In the placement process the acknowledgment of participants special developmental tasks should include normalizing the possible need for postadoption services. These services might include individual or family counseling, peer support groups, provision of information about current laws and practices, and contact with intermediaries regarding ongoing pertinent information. Services may also include legal interventions. Birth parents or adoptive parents may find that the original contract is unworkable in some way, particularly with children's changing developmental needs. One or both parties may request a shift in the contract toward more or less contact. Such requests for shifts must be dealt with respectfully and must be considered part of the development of the adoptive family circle.

Surrounding the adoption circle are professionals involved in setting adoption laws and practices. Here there needs to be a continuing commitment to learning more about the adoption circle through evaluation and research, teaching what is known through consultation and training programs, networking of resources, and working toward social and legal reforms based on the current state of knowledge.

Even as we attempt to change in the best ways we now know, we must remember the earnest policy setters 20 years ago whom we now criticize so righteously. We must think ahead 20 years from now to those who will undoubtedly believe we were equally remiss in our judgments. Those who struggle to understand and act on behalf of this alternative family can take pride in contributing to a knowledge base on adoption that can be used to improve the lives of those within the adoption family circle.

AFTERWORD

IT IS HUMAN NATURE TO want and to expect our lives to proceed along the course we have defined as the way it is "supposed to be." Such wishes and expectations have not been met for members of the adoption circle. Except for surrogate mothers, no one plans to have a baby and relinquish it. No one chooses infertility, though some may prefer adoption over childbearing. No one wishes for birth parents who are not in a position to competently and lovingly raise them. For some members of the circle, the necessity of adoption may signify a loss of innocence; this may be their first confrontation with life circumstances that are not the way they are "supposed to be."

It is also human nature to want and to expect one's pain to be remedied and to feel that some kind of reparation is due. Adoption is a social institution that is designed to offer restitution: birth parents are provided with eager alternative parents for their child, adopting parents are provided with a child for whom they have longed, and children are povided with welcoming homes. Yet with this restitution comes the paradox all adoption circle members must accept: the difference between their biological and their functional relationships. We have seen that adoption does not erase the wishes of its participants. Birth parents wish they could have been in a position to keep and raise their child. Adoptive parents wish they could have borne the child they raised. Adoptees wish their birth and rearing parents were one and the same couple. We have also seen that members of the adoption circle are faced with special developmental tasks and that the tasks of each member interact with those of other members—in fantasy or in reality—over the entire life course. There is wide variation in members' abilities to master these tasks sufficiently to feel satisfied with their experiences.

The clinical, social, and legal agents who surround the adoption circle struggle to develop the best possible ways of enhancing the experiences of its members. In the last decade there has been a high value placed on confronting the "as if" atmosphere that previously had been encouraged in adoption practices. Many note the dangers, discussed in this book, of denying the realities of being a birth parent, adoptive parent, or adoptee. Some recommend new procedures and policies, particularly openness, to help with the confrontation of these realities. In time, we may find that such openness works effectively for some or many adoption circles. However, the full range of personalities and experiences we observe in the adoption circle requires us to respect individual and family differences and to offer and support a full range of coping strategies.

As with all types of families, there will be varying degrees of success and gratification for adoptive family members. There is no guarantee that all members' needs will be met or that their pain will be salved. The measure of success, therefore, is not the absence of struggle and pain. Rather, success in adoption is the achievement of the family structure that meets the needs of its participants more fully than its alternatives. Successful adoption circles thrive on the bonds of mutual love and respect that transcend blood ties. These genuine feelings give members of the circle the strength and the ability to embrace the challenges of adoptive family life. Birth parents, adoptive parents, and adoptees can then take special pleasure in being part of the mastery of these essential human struggles.

DEVELOPMENTAL TASKS OF BIRTH PARENTS

Phase	Goals/Tasks	Emotional Issues
Decision to Relinquish	Making decision to place child for adoption	Accepting responsibility for pregnancy (guilt/shame)
		Resolving ambivalence toward fetus
		Attachment and loss
Preparation for Adoption	Making legal arrangements	Coping with separation through birth
	Relinquishing parental rights	Coming to terms with own and other's feelings about relinquishment

The charts in Appendixes A through C are modeled after those in *The Family Life Cycle,* ed. B. Carter and M. McGoldrick (New York: Gardner Press, 1980).

APPENDIX A　Developmental Tasks of Birth Parents (Continued)

Phase	Goals/Tasks	Emotional Issues
		Resolving fantasies/fears regarding competence of adopting parents vs. own competence
Adoption	Relinquishing physical possession Deciding type of adoption and amount of contact with adoptive parents and child	Mourning process: realization, alarm, searching, anger and guilt (self-reproach), loss of self, identification
Postadoption Middle Years	Resuming life pursuits Carrying out or renegotiating adoption contract	Continued mourning Coping with fantasies of search and restitution and coping with fear of secret being revealed Forgiving self and others Dealing with impact on child's other biological parent, sexual relationships, relationship(s) with kept child(ren)
Later Life	Deciding to search or be found Accepting relinquishment with tranquility	Periodic mourning Accepting possibility of unknown grandchildren Dealing with realities of birthchild, if contact made

DEVELOPMENTAL TASKS OF ADOPTIVE PARENTS

Phase	Goals/Tasks	Emotional Issues
Decision for Adoption to Take Place	Accepting inability to reproduce successfully	Acceptance of one's or spouse's failure to reproduce successfully
	Deciding to parent children outside of bloodline	Differentiation between reproduction, sexual adequacy, and competence to parent
	Deciding on type of adoption	Dealing with spouse and extended family about genealogical discontinuity
Adoption Process	Making social and legal arrangements	Accepting need to open up to public scrutiny

(continued)

APPENDIX B Developmental Tasks of Adoptive Parents
(Continued)

Phase	Goals/Tasks	Emotional Issues
		Seeking social validation of parenting competence
		Mourning loss of bloodline
Adoption	Accepting new member into the family	Mourning loss of fantasized biological child
		Adjusting to instant parenthood
		Accepting "ghosts" of biological parents and their families as part of constitution of the family
		Bonding with child
		Acceptance of psychological parenthood (vs. biological parenthood)
		Realignment of relationships with extended family to accept nonbiological child
		Dealing with community attitudes toward adoption
Adoptive Parents with Pre-school Child	Acknowledging adoption as a fact of family life	Testing permanency of relationship
	Disclosure of adoption: to tell or not tell: who, when, what, and how to tell?	Dealing with responses to news of adoption

Phase	Goals/Tasks	Emotional Issues
Adoptive Parents with School-Aged Child	Acknowledging of adoption as a fact of family life in wider community	Dealing with child's wish/fear of biological parent's contact and own concerns about being good enough Dealing with child's ambivalence/splitting anxiety about being "returned" Dealing with community reactions to the adoptive status of child
Adoptive Parents with Adolescent	Increasing flexibility of family boundaries Accepting a different model of family (psychological vs. genetic bonding) Accepting child's identity as combination of biological base and adoptive upbringing Maintenance of sexual boundaries in the absence of firm incest taboo	Separation–individuation issues: achieving independence, not eviction Differenting between nuclear family and triadic family Accepting adolescent's interest in biological family as a help in the development of a stable identity Accepting child's struggle with sexual identity issues and child's images of biological vs. adoptive parents Recontracting: accepting adoption again

(continued)

APPENDIX B   Developmental Tasks of Adoptive Parents
(Continued)

Phase	Goals/Tasks	Emotional Issues
Adoptive Parents with Young Adult	Accepting a multitude of exits from and entries into the family system	Dealing with young adult's ability to reproduce and attach to blood relative
	Dealing with issues of search for biological parents	Reaffirmation of ties within adoptive family
		Mourning lack of fantasized biological child
Adoptive Parents in Later Life	Accepting shifting of generational roles	Dealing with genealogical discontinuity
	Accepting adoptive circumstances with tranquility	Mourning of biological progeny and recognizing psychological inheritance
		Mortality

DEVELOPMENTAL TASKS OF ADOPTEES

Phase	Goals/Tasks	Emotional Issues
Preadoption		
Conception, Pregnancy and Birth	Survival	Circumstances of genetic base, prenatal and natal experience, and temperament
Postpartum	Surviving trauma of maternal–child separation(s) and displacement(s)	Separation and loss Shift(s) in environment

(continued)

APPENDIX C Developmental Tasks of Adoptees (Continued)

Phase	Goals/Tasks	Emotional Issues
Adoption		
Infancy	Recovering from trauma of separation Bonding with adoptive parents	Attachment
Preschool	Developing trust Developing initiative and autonomy while maintaining attachment to parents Integrating "news" of adoption if told at this time	Aggression and self-control Self-esteem and attachment
School-Aged Child	Developing competence at various pursuits Integrating "news" of adoption if told at this time Affirming permanency of family	Recognition of having two sets of parents and dealing with ambivalence toward both Struggling with anxiety regarding permanency of adoptive relationship Struggling with self-esteem related to feelings of abandonment
Puberty and Adolescence	Confronting genetic and psychological parts of self Accepting different model of family	Sexuality Identifications Interest in biological family

Phase	Goals/Tasks	Emotional Issues
	Forming an identity that integrates biology and upbringing	Struggling with ambivalence/splitting regarding two sets of parents and beginning to recontract.
	Achieving independence rather than eviction	Separation–individuation
Young Adult	Coming to terms with genealogy in order to make choices regarding new family and career	Genealogical continuity
		Continued interest in biological family and possible search
	Seeking intimate relationship (screening out possible biological relatives as mates)	
	Recontracting and reaffirming ties with adoptive family on basis of acceptance of triadic family.	
	Deciding to search or not	
Adulthood	Procreation of blood children	Accepting shift in generational roles
	Guiding new generation with sense of integration of one's own biological and psychological past	
	Disclosing one's adoption to own children	

(continued)

APPENDIX C Developmental Tasks of Adoptees (Continued)

Phase	Goals/Tasks	Emotional Issues
Later Life	Acceptance of one's life experience with sense of cohesion and integrity	Mortality

NOTES

CHAPTER 1:   The Myth of the Perfect Solution

1. A. Baran and R. Pannor on a panel entitled "Sharpening the Focus" at the 13th International Conference of the American Adoption Congress, Garden Grove, Calif., 11, April 1991.
2. A. Landers, Los Angeles Times/Creaters Syndicates, 5, July 1991.
3. *New York Times*, 10, July 1991. "Tough Adoptions: New York Tries 'Hard Sell'"
4. K. Dukakis with J. Scovell, *Now You Know* (New York: Simon & Schuster, 1990).
5. L. Caplan, *An Open Adoption* (New York: Farrar, Straus & Giroux, 1990).
6. A. Haley, *Roots* (Garden City, N.Y.: Doubleday, 1976).
7. A. Kraft, J. Palombo, P. Woods, D. Mitchell, and A. Schmidt, "Some Theoretical Considerations on Confidential Adoptions: Part III. The Adopted Child," *Child and Adolescent Social Work* 2 (1985): 139–153.
8. A. Kraft, J. Palombo, P. Woods, D. Mitchell, and A. Schmidt, "Some Theoretical Considerations on Confidential Adoptions: Part II. The Adoptive Parent," *Child and Adolescent Social Work,* 2 (1985): 69–81.
9. A. Kraft, J. Palombo, P. Woods, D. Mitchell, and A. Schmidt, "Some Theoretical Considerations on Confidential Adoptions: Part I. The Birth Mother," *Child and Adolescent Social Work,* 2 (1985): 13–21.
10. A. Baran and R. Pannor at the 13th International Conference of the American Adoption Congress, Garden Grove, Cal., 11, April 1991.

CHAPTER 2:   To Have but Not to Hold

1. L. Millen and S. Roll, "Solomon's Mothers: A Special Case of Pathological Bereavement," *American Journal of Orthopsychiatry* 55 (1985): 411–418.

2. For a fine overview, see A. B. Brodzinsky, "Surrendering an Infant for Adoption," in *The Psychology of Adoption*, ed. D. M. Brodzinsky and M. D. Schechter (New York: Oxford University Press, 1990).

3. C. A. Bachrach, "Adoption Plans, Adopted Children, and Adoptive Mothers," *Journal of Marriage and the Family*, 48 (1986): 243–253.

4. A. Washington, "A Cultural and Historical Perspective on Pregnancy-Related Activity Among U.S. Teenagers," *Journal of Black Psychology* 9 (1982): 1–28.

5. J. G. Dryfoos and R. Lincoln, *Teenage Pregnancy: The Problem That Hasn't Gone Away* (New York: Alan Guttmacher Institute, 1981).

6. E. Y. Deykin, L. Campbell and P. Patti, "The Postadoption Experience of Surrendering Parents," *American Journal of Orthopsychiatry* 54 (1984): 271–280.

7. Bachrach, "Adoption Plans."

8. J. M. Horn and R. G. Turner, "Minnesota Multiphasic Personality Inventory Profiles among Subgroups of Unwed Mothers," *Journal of Consulting and Clinical Psychology"* 44 (1976): 25–33.

9. B. Plain, *Blessings* (New York: Delacorte Press, 1989).

10. L. Caplan, *An Open Adoption* (New York: Farrar, Straus & Giroux, 1990).

11. S. Gold-Steinberg, "Legal and Illegal Abortion: Coping with the Impact of Social Policies on Women's Lives" (unpublished diss. University of Michigan, 1991).

12. Caplan, *Open Adoption.*

13. Millen and Roll, "Solomon's Mothers."

14. Plain, *Blessings.*

15. J. Gediman and L. Brown, *Birthbond* (Far Hills, N.J.: New Horizons Press, 1989).

16. E. K. Rynearson, "Relinquishment and its Maternal Complications: A Preliminary Study," *American Journal of Psychiatry* 139 (1982): 338–340.

17. Millen and Roll, "Solomon's Mothers."

18. A. Sorosky, A. Baran and R. Pannor, *The Adoption Triangle* (New York: Doubleday, 1978).

19. Deykin, Campbell, and Patti, "Surrendering Parents."

20. R. Winkler and M. van Keppel, *Relinquishing Mothers in Adoption: Their Long-Term Adjustment* (Melbourne: Institute of Family Studies, 1984).

21. E. Y. Deykin, P. Patti, and J. Ryan, "Fathers of Adopted Children: A

Study of the Impact of Child Surrender on Birthfathers," *American Journal of Orthopsychiatry* 58 (1988): 240–248.

CHAPTER 3: Becoming Parents

1. H. D. Kirk, *Shared Fate* (New York: Free Press, 1964).

2. A. Sorosky, A. Baran, and R. Pannor, *The Adoption Triangle* (New York: Doubleday, 1978).

3. D. Renne, "There's Always Adoption: The Infertility Problem," *Child Welfare* 56 (1977): 465–470.

4. F. M. Andrews, "Psychological Aspects of Infertility," (Unpublished study, University of Michigan, 1990).

5. S. Chess and A. Thomas, *Temperament and Development* (New York: Brunner/Mazel, 1977).

6. L. M. Singer, D. M. Brodzinsky, D. Ramsay, M. Steir, and E. Waters, "Mother–Infant Attachment in Adoptive Families," *Child Development* 56 (1985): 1543–1551.

7. J. Triseliotis and J. Russell, *Hard to Place* (London: Glower, 1984).

8. A. Kadushin, *Adopting Older Children* (New York: Columbia University Press, 1970).

9. B. Tizard, *Adoption: A Second Chance* (London: Open Books, 1977).

10. J. Lamb and S. Leurgans, "Does Adoption Affect Subsequent Fertility?" *American Journal of Obstetrics and Gynecology* 134 (1979): 138–144.

11. B. Bettelheim, at a mother's meeting, Chicago, 1970.

12. V. Wasson, *The Chosen Baby* (Philadelphia: Lippincott, 1939).

13. T. B. Brazelton, *Families: Crisis and Caring* (Reading, Mass.: Addison-Wesley, 1989).

14. D. M. Brodzinsky, L. M. Singer, and A. M. Braff, "Children's Understanding of Adoption," *Child Development* 55 (1984): 869–878.

15. J. L. Pickar, "Children's Understanding of Parenthood," (Unpublished diss., University of Michigan, 1986).

16. P. McCullough, "Launching Children and Moving On," in *The Family Life Cycle,* ed. B. Carter and M. McGoldrick (New York: Gardner Press, 1980).

17. Ibid., 172.

18. Ibid., 177.

19. Kirk, *Shared Fate.*

20. D. M. Brodzinsky, "A Stress and Coping Model of Adoption Adjustment" in *The Psychology of Adoption,* ed. D. M. Brodzinsky and M. D. Schechter (New York: Oxford University Press, 1990).

CHAPTER 4: Growing Up Adopted

1. For a full discussion, see R. Cadoret, "Biologic Perspectives of Adoptee Adjustment," in *The Psychology of Adoption*, ed. D. M. Brodzinsky and M. D. Schechter (New York: Oxford Unviersity Press, 1990).

2. S. Fraiberg, *The Magic Years* (New York: Scribner, 1959).

3. J. Piaget, *The Child's Conception of the World* (Paterson, N.J.: Littlefield, Adams and Co., 1963).

4. E. Erickson, *Childhood and Society* (New York: Norton, 1950).

5. L. H. Campbell, P. R. Silverman, P. B. Patti, "Reunions Between Adoptees and Birthparents: The Adoptees' Experience," *Social Work* 36 (1991): 329–335.

6. S. Aumend and M. Barrett, "Self-Concept and Attitudes Toward Adoption: A Comparison of Searching and Non-Searching Adult Adoptees," *Child Welfare* 63 (1984): 251–259.

7. J. Triseliotis, *In Search of Origins* (London: Routledge and Kegan Paul, 1973).

8. Campbell, Silverman, and Patti, "Reunions," 334.

9. A. Sorosky, A. Baran and R. Pannor, *The Adoption Triangle* (New York: Doubleday, 1978, revised 1984).

10. P. Brinich, "Some Potential Effects of Adoption on Self and Object Representations," *Psychoanalytic Study of the Child* 37 (1980): 107–133.

11. E. Rosenberg and T. Horner, "Birthparent Romances and Identity Formation in Adopted Children," *American Journal of Orthopsychiatry* 61 (1991): 70–77.

12. Sorosky, Baran, and Pannor, *Adoption Triangle*.

13. M. Schechter, P. V. Carlson, J. Q. Simmons and H. H. Work, "Emotional Problems of the Adoptee," *Archives of General Psychiatry* 10 (1964): 37–46.

14. P. Toussieng, "Thoughts Regarding the Etiology of Psychological Difficulties in Adopted Children," *Child Welfare* 41 (1962): 59–65.

15. A. Elonen and E. Schwartz, "A Longitudinal Study of Emotional, Social and Academic Functioning of Adopted Children," *Child Welfare* 48 (1969): 72–78.

16. J. L. Hoopes, *Prediction in Child Development: A Longitudinal Study of Adoptive and Nonadoptive Families* (New York: Child Welfare League of America, 1982).

17. M. Bohman, *Adopted Children and Their Families* (Stockholm: Proprius, 1970).

18. B. W. Lindholm and J. Touliatus, "Psychological Adjustment of Adopted and Non-adopted Children," *Psychological Reports* 46 (1980): 307–310.

19. D. M. Brodzinsky, C. Radice, L. Huffman and K. Merkler, "Prevalence of Clinically Significant Symptomatology in a Nonclinical Sample of Adopted and Nonadopted Children," *Journal of Clinical Child Psychology* 16 (1987): 350–356.

20. M. Norvell and R. F. Guy, "A Comparison of Self-Concept in Adopted and Nonadopted Adolescents," *Adolescence* 12 (1977): 443–448.

21. W. W. Simmons, "A Study of Identity Formation in Adoptees," *Dissertation Abstracts International*, 40, 12-B Part 1, 5832.

22. L. Stein and J. Hoopes, *Identity Formation in the Adopted Adolescents* (New York: Child Welfare League of America, 1985).

CHAPTER 5: Shared Lives

1. A. J. Ferreira, "Family Myth and Homeostasis," *Archives of General Psychiatry* 9 (1963): 55.

2. L. M. Singer, D. M. Brodzinsky, D. Ramsay et al., "Mother–Infant Attachment in Adoptive Families," *Child Development* 56 (1985): 1543–1551.

3. P. Sachdev, *Unlocking the Adoption Files* (Lexington, Mass.: Lexington Books, 1989).

4. Sachdev, *Unlocking Files.*

CHAPTER 6: When Help Is Needed

1. M. McGoldrick and R. Gerson, *Genograms in Family Assessment* (New York: Norton, 1985).

2. A. Hartman, *Working with Adoptive Families Beyond Placement* (New York: Child Welfare League of America, 1984).

3. R. C. Winkler, D. W. Brown, M. van Keppel, and A. Blanchard, *Clinical Practice in Adoption* (New York: Pergamon Press, 1988).

4. L. Coleman, K. Tilbor, H. Hornby, and C. Boaals, *Working with Older Adoptees* (Portland, Maine: University of Southern Maine, 1988).

5. L. C. Berman and R. K. Bufferd, "Family Treatment to Address Loss in Adoptive Families," *Social Casework* 67 (1986): 3–11.

CHAPTER 7: Surrounding the Adoption Circle

1. E. S. Cole and K. S. Donley, "History, Values, and Placement Policy Issues in Adoption," in *The Psychology of Adoption*, ed. D. W. Brod-

zinsky and M. D. Schechter (New York: Oxford University Press, 1990).

2. J. Goldstein, A. Freud, and A. Solnit, *Beyond the Best Interests of the Child* (London: Free Press, 1973).

3. J. Goldstein, A. Freud, and A. Solnit, *Before the Best Interests of the Child* (New York: Free Press, 1979).

4. Child Welfare League of America, *Standards for Adoption Service*, rev. ed. (New York: CWLA, 1978).

5. Child Welfare, *Standards*.

6. K. A. Nelson, *On the Frontier of Adoption: A Study of Special Needs Adoptive Families* (Washington, D.C.: Child Welfare League of America, 1985).

7. A. Sorosky, A. Baran, and R. Pannor, *The Adoption Triangle*, rev. ed. (New York: Doubleday, 1984).

8. Child Welfare, *Standards*.

9. Child Welfare, *Standards*.

10. Sorosky, Baran, and Pannor, *Adoption Triangle*.

11. A. Hartman, *Finding Families* (Beverly Hills, Cal.: Sage, 1979).

12. I am indebted to Joan Hollinger, Professor of Law at the University of Detroit School of Law for her generous sharing of knowledge of adoption laws and practices. Most of the information reported here was culled from her presentation at the 13th International Meeting of the American Adoption Congress in 1991, Garden Grove, California, her writings in *Adoption Law and Practices* (1988, supp. 1989, 1990, 1991), which she also edits, and her presentation at the Family Therapy Seminar at the University of Michigan Department of Child Psychiatry, 1991. Professor Hollinger is also the reporter for the proposed Uniform Adoption Act, referred to in the text.

13. P. Sachdev, *Unlocking the Adoption Files* (Lexington, Mass.: Lexington Books, 1989).

14. J. S. Gediman and L. P. Brown, *Birthbond* (Far Hills, N.J.: New Horizon Press, 1989).

15. R. Pannor and A. Baran on a panel entitled "Sharpening the Focus" at the 13th International Conference of the American Adoption Congress, Garden Grove, Calif., 11 April 1991.

16. J. Demick and S. Wapner, "Open and Closed Adoptions: A Developmental conceptualization," *Family Process* 27 (1988): 229–249.

17. R. G. McRoy, H. D. Grotevant, and K. L. White, *Openness in Adoption: New Practices, New Issues* (New York: Praeger, 1988).

INDEX